Was GOD on Vacation?

A WWII AUTOBIOGRAPHY

D1248874

*I dedicate this book to the brave men
who stormed the beaches of Normandy on
June 6, 1944, and to the heroes of the
biggest battle of this century, the
Battle of the Bulge.*
                              Jack van der Geest

Jack van der Geest

Introduction

OR FORTY YEARS following World War II, I was unable to talk about my concentration camp experiences except with my wife. I couldn't relive the brutalities I'd endured, the fear, the atrocities I'd been forced to perform, the hunger, the sleepless nights. A school teacher's statement changed all of that for me. When she said, "There never was a Holocaust," something exploded within me. I had to prove to her and to other doubters that absolutely the Holocaust was real. It was then that I began to write the memoirs of my concentration camp and World War II experiences.

I'd lived in the U.S. for many years by this time, and could comprehend how difficult it might be for an American surrounded with abundance to understand living through the Holocaust. I understood how some people could find it hard to believe what it was like to live in a country under occupation: the hunger, the indignities, the restriction of movement, the terror of having the front door kicked in and being dragged away to a concentration camp without reason or a trial. I set out, through my memoirs, to help erase the doubt in anyone's mind that the Holocaust was a horrible reality.

Now as a fifty year resident of the U.S., forty-six years as a citizen, I have enjoyed every minute of my most precious possession—freedom. I am reminded of the immigrant who walked into a cafeteria in New York. He sat down to be waited on. An American told him, "Go through the line, take what you want and pay at the end."

That is the real way to have a life of freedom in America. Roll up your sleeves, pitch in and don't sit there waiting for a hand-out.

Acknowledgments

It is with deep gratitude that I acknowledge the people who were instrumental in getting this book into print. I would like to thank my wonderful wife, Elaine. Without her encouragement and support, I never would have begun to write this book. Second, I would like to thank the many people who heard my speeches and encouraged me to write my story. I would like to express my appreciation to Carol Ordemann who brought my book to life through her expertise and knowledge. Her enthusiasm and drive to get this book into print were astronomical. I am grateful to my son, Van, for the thoughts, ideas, and contacts he shared with me in his efforts to complete this project. Last, but not least, I would like to thank my readers for taking the time to read my story, a story that needed to be told. A story that is not yet in our history books, but should be!

Jack van der Geest

EDITOR'S NOTE: There was no doubt in my mind after reading Jack's memoirs that this was a story that must be told. Sitting with Jack for hours taping and writing out details to supplement his memoirs, I shared his feelings as I heard his voice crack with emotion and saw the tears in his eyes. As I rewrote his words into a story I experienced his anguish with him. Several nights I dreamed I was a prisoner in a concentration camp. At times I became so overwhelmed with writing his experiences that I turned off my computer and went for a long walk. This is truly a story that must be brought to the public.

I would like to thank my family and friends for their support and encouragement during this year-long project. A huge thanks goes to my writing critique group for their patience, care and suggestions through my many rewrites. We are all indebted to Jack for opening up his life to share with the world. He showed a lot of courage, fortitude and cooperation in telling his story, in answering my many questions, and in going over my rewrites. And thanks to Jack's son Van for understanding the importance of his father's story and for seeing that it was published.

Carol J. Ordemann

Jack van der Geest, age 7 (1930)
with grandfather William de Groot

Preface

"GOD MADE THE WORLD, but the Dutch made Holland," is a saying the Dutch are fond of quoting. When many people hear the word *Holland*, they think of the little country on the North Sea with the tulips, dikes, windmills, Gouda cheese and many bicycles. But what most people call Holland is really The Netherlands. The Netherlands, meaning lowlands, is made up of eleven provinces, two of which are North Holland and South Holland. Because Amsterdam is in North Holland and Rotterdam in South Holland, and a large percentage of the population live in these two provinces, The Netherlands is often referred to as Holland.

The Netherlands is a monarchy, and at the time of this story was ruled by Queen Wilhelmina, whose husband Prince Hendrik had died in 1934. In 1938 Queen Wilhelmina celebrated her Fortieth Anniversary as ruler of The Netherlands, and the Dutch enthusiastically joined her in the festivities. There was much to celebrate—the Dutch were prosperous and free. They had a history to be proud of, seafarers who had explored the world, painters such as Rembrandt and Van Gogh to represent them.

Even though The Netherlands is a small country—seventy-five miles across and one hundred fifty miles long, with a population of 11,000,000 before World War II—she had to fight many wars in the past to stay independent. Ironically, several wars had been fought with England, and one ninety-year war with Spain. In the Twentieth century The Netherlands adopted a policy of neutrality and managed to stay out of World War I.

Maybe this was the reason the Dutch people did not get overly excited when Hitler came to power, built a tremendous army navy, and air force and began making war on European countries.

NETHERLANDS

Amsterdam

Scheveningen The Hague

Rotterdam

Maastricht

CHAPTER I

Invasion of
The Netherlands

TARTLED AWAKE BY THE BOOM and flash of gunfire, I groped for the lamp switch and pulled the cord. "Hey, Fred. What's going on?" I asked groggily. I checked my clock, "It isn't even 4:00 AM."

Fred crooked his elbow over his eyes and groaned. Fred de Koning stayed with me week nights to attend The Netherlands Aircraft Institute in Scheveningen near The Hague where I lived.

I leaped out of bed, shook Fred's shoulder and slipped on a pair of pants and a shirt. "Come on Fred, let's go see." Not even Fred could have slept through the explosions outside. Fred jumped up, dragged his fingers through his dark hair and dressed quickly. We ran into the hall and bumped into Ma, Pa and my older sister, Willie. Together we rushed downstairs and into the street in front of our apartment building south of The Hague.

In the pink half-light of dawn we stared open mouthed as German Stukas crisscrossed the sky, screeching into dives to drop their bombs. It looked as if the Germans were bombing Amsterdam, about thirty miles northeast of us. Families from ours and neighboring apartment houses crowded the street and pointed and exclaimed at what seem to Fred and me like an air show.

"This looks like a newsreel of the bombing of Poland," I said,

"I was thinking the same thing," commented Fred.

"My God, I hope they aren't bombing houses," said Ma, her arthritic hands gripping my father's arm.

"I'd guess their target is the Amsterdam airport," said Pa, squeezing her hands.

Suddenly, a huge flame shot from the tail of a circling Stuka. "Look," I shouted. "Our Air Force just shot down a German plane." The plane hung suspended then nose dived to the ground about two blocks from where we stood.

Children cheered while adults animatedly discussed the situation.

"Do you think the German Blitzkrieg is attacking The Netherlands?" asked an elderly neighbor, disbelief written on his lined face.

"How could that be?" asked a retired banker who lived downstairs. "The Netherlands was neutral in World War I and Queen Wilhelmina guaranteed we'd stay neutral in this war. Why, just the other day she wrote in the paper that our country didn't possess anything of value to the Germans."

"And did you hear the Prime Minister on the radio just last night assuring us that the Germans would respect the neutrality of the Dutch?" a French cook asked angrily.

While adults questioned what had happened, young children "oohed" and "ahhed." I didn't know what to think, but felt more excited than worried.

The answers to our questions were not long in coming. Within half an hour a flight of fifteen to twenty Stukas appeared. Now in daylight we clearly saw the black swastika emblems against the gray of the tails and undersides of the wings. Bundles of pamphlets dropped from the planes and floated to the earth. I caught a sheet and eagerly read.

"WE THE GERMAN PEOPLE CAME TO LIBERATE YOU"

The message, written in Dutch and German, was appropriately bordered in black and red, Nazi colors.

In the short time between the two German forays over Holland, Fred and I stayed outside while Pa, Ma and Willie went back into our apartment to listen to the emergency frequency on our radio.

"Mark my word," Pa said before leaving, "May 10, 1940 will be a day never to be forgotten by the Dutch." When he returned outside he reported, "I couldn't receive any information. Both radio stations are dead."

After the leaflet drop, the skies over The Hague grew quiet. Fred and I felt little concern about the Germans, and he asked me to come home with him for the weekend. This was something we did frequently and my parents agreed to it, with warnings that we be careful. As boys of sixteen, we had long been allowed to bicycle to Fred's home in Rotterdam, a city located eighteen miles southeast of The Hague. School had been canceled for the day so Fred and I left for Rotterdam as soon as possible.

Saturday, while I was at the de Konings, the radio stations came back on the air. Fred, his mother, father and I crowded around their standing cherrywood radio and listened to a Dutch broadcaster announce, "Germany has invaded The Netherlands. Try to stay calm..."

Still no one seemed overly alarmed. The following day the radio reported that The Netherlands Army had opened dikes on the southeastern corner of our country. By flooding the farmland and planting barbed wire in the water they hoped to keep the German Army, which had massed on our eastern border, from crossing into The Netherlands.

"For many years in the past," explained Fred, a history buff, "this method was used successfully to keep enemies from invading our territory."

Flooding farmlands worked against foot soldiers and horses, I thought, *but would it work against soldier driven tanks?*

Usually Fred and I would return to my home on Sunday after enjoying a Saturday night of dancing at one of our favorite dance halls in Rotterdam. But since schools would remain closed on Monday, we decided instead to prolong my weekend visit.

Monday went by uneventfully. Only a few German planes flew over, acting as nonaggressive as those of the Dutch Air Force. So on Tuesday, May 14th, Fred and I agreed to bicycle into downtown Rotterdam, where there was always plenty of activity. It was early afternoon of what seemed like a normal business day. Streets flowed with cars, Trams and bicycles. Sidewalks were crowded with businessmen, shoppers and children enjoying yet another free day from school.

We ended up on De Coolsingel, the main thoroughfare of Rotterdam, a street that is ten lanes wide. A sidewalk lined by stores runs along one side, then two bicycle lanes, two car lanes, and streetcar tracks all going south. A safety zone separated these lanes from the five northbound lanes. Another sidewalk and stores lined the other side.

We pedaled south down the bike lane toward a big department store that covered one entire block, called De Bijenkorf, the beehive. It had probably been given that nickname because of the large numbers of people streaming in and out of its many entrances and exits.

Just at the time we approached De Bijenkorf, German airplanes screamed overhead out of nowhere and started to bomb Rotterdam. I looked up and saw and heard the beehive's many large windows vibrating. "Let's get the hell out of here," I yelled.

Fred and I, pushing our bikes, dashed across the ten lanes of traffic and hid in the entryway of a jewelry store on the other side. The windows and door of the store, recessed three or four feet, were covered with wrought iron screens. As we huddled shaking in the entryway, we saw the beehive take a direct hit from a bomb that completely flattened the huge building. Only the screens covering the windows of the jewelry store prevented its exploding glass from carving us to pieces.

German Stukas continued to dive from the sky as they dropped bombs over the city. Traffic screeched to a halt. Between explosions I heard the cries and moans of injured people trapped under the rubble of the beehive and other bombed out buildings.

A survivor shouted, "Get over here and help. People are dying."

Fred and I left our bicycles and raced back to the rubble of the beehive to assist. That move saved our lives. Moments after we'd recrossed the ten lanes, we turned to see a bomb explode on the building where the jewelry store was located. "God must have been watching our for us," I mumbled.

During the one and one half hours of bombing and after, Fred and I joined the many volunteers freeing people from the debris. Some people were only bruised, but others were brought out severely wounded or dead. The stench of blood, vomit, excrement and death turned my stomach. I had to focus on the task before me to keep from running away. Before long, bodies lined the sidewalk awaiting aid from rescuers who were long in coming because of all the damage to streets and buildings. Nighttime forced rescue efforts to a halt.

We hadn't looked for Fred's family because of our intense involvement with the rescue. Fred asked someone where we could find survivors. He directed us to the woods south of town, a designated meeting area in case of an emergency. It became a night we'd never forget. Hundreds of people gathered there to search for lost ones; mothers carrying babies called out for husbands, parents for children.

Fred's father, who worked downtown, was not there so we made our way back to the city center. We found our bikes, and though they were banged up we rode them to Fred's house in north Rotterdam. By this time it was early morning and daylight filtered through the heavy, dusty air. Nothing was left of his house except the foundation. Fred's face went pale and his scraped and bleeding hands gripped the handlebars of his bike as he stared wordlessly into the bomb hole that used to be his home. His shoulders sagged and tears filled his eyes.

"Let's go to Marie's apartment," he choked out.

We biked to his married sister's place. To our great relief, we found her still in her damaged, but livable, quarters. Unbelievably, Fred's mother was also there and unharmed. She had been visiting when the bombing started.

With tears streaming down her cheeks, his mother threw her arms around us. "I'm so glad you're safe. I thought you were both dead,"

Fred blinked fast to keep his tears from overflowing. "Mother, our house has been totally destroyed. Nothing is left."

"Fred, your father. Did you see him?" she asked, seeming not to have heard about their home.

"No. He wasn't at the emergency site south of the city."

With Fred's father still unaccounted for, the four of us split into two teams to look for him. Fred's mother and sister checked with friends and relatives while Fred and I returned downtown where his father worked as an accountant. My stomach sank when I saw the building where his father's office had been located. I looked into Fred's eyes and knew that we both felt there was little hope that his father had survived. Later that day we were informed that Fred's father had perished in the raid. His body was never identified. In shock, Fred, his mother, sister and I joined the many who grieved for the estimated 900 lost in the bombing of Rotterdam. In this German "horror raid" we later learned that 25,000 houses had been destroyed and 78,000 people left homeless.

It was Wednesday, May 15th, only five days after German planes had dropped the fliers that announced they planned to liberate The Netherlands, when a frightening bulletin came over the radio. A Dutch newscaster relayed this message for the Germans: "IF THE DUTCH PEOPLE DO NOT SURRENDER, THE NEXT CITY TO BE BOMBED WILL BE THE HAGUE AND THE NEXT AMSTERDAM."

This announcement became the turning point for every person living in The Netherlands! Though I hated to leave my best friend Fred, I felt I had to get back home. My family greeted me with tears of relief. Sadly I told them about Mr. de Koning's death in the bombing of Rotterdam. Almost everyone we knew had been touched by the death of a friend or relative. Now we who lived in The Hague worried that our city would be devastated in the same way that Rotterdam had been.

Pa, expressing his typical anti-royalist sentiments, said, "This goes to show you, you can't trust the queen. She promised this wouldn't happen."

We were finally forced to admit to ourselves that The Netherlands was at war. With the small armed forces of our country, there was not a prayer that we could protect ourselves. The Netherlands had no choice but to surrender.

She did.

That very same day.

CHAPTER II

Occupation— German Hold Tightens

T HE NEXT DAY MY FAMILY, neighbors and I waited to find out what would happen. Excitedly I called Ma, Pa and Willie to our third floor, living room window to see a long line of limousines and cars speed down the "Hoek van Holland" from The Hague toward Rotterdam. The motorcade was out of sight before anyone could identify the dignitaries, but it was not long before we figured out that it was Queen Wilhelmina, her royal family and staff. Later we learned that the British Navy waited at the seaport to take the royal family to England, where they remained throughout the war. Their desertion left many Dutch people angry and confused.

"That's about what I would expect of our queen," commented Pa.

Within hours, almost before the dust had settled from the departure of Queen Wilhelmina, a German convoy drove into town accompanied by a long line of tanks and trucks filled with soldiers and equipment. The German forces were well organized. They circled for several blocks, the first vehicle closing in on the last. I thought that the whole German Army had arrived until I recognized one of the vehicles that had passed by before.

Finally the convoy came to a halt. German soldiers jumped down and handed out candy saying, "Remember, we've come to liberate you."

The question, "From what?" passed through my mind.

After trying to make a good first impression, the Moffen—Dutch profanity for German soldiers—dispersed in small groups. Some of them bought, meaning helped themselves to, bread from the bakery, hamburger from the meat shop and onions and cream from the produce and dairy stores.

I stared from the curb as the soldiers mixed the raw meat, onions and cream together then slapped it onto a slice of bread. To my amazement they ate this concoction as if it were a royal banquet. My first opinion was that they must be cannibals.

All over Holland this scene was repeated. While some soldiers ate, others dispersed to take over warehouses, radio stations, city halls and government offices. In a few hours the Germans were in full control. The soldiers confiscated all our guns. It wasn't hard to do. By a Dutch law passed in 1938, gun owners had to register their weapons at City Hall. The Queen had left the list behind in her rush to safety.

Our own weapons were taken away late that Thursday afternoon. A knock sounded on our apartment door. Ma and I were the only ones at home. Pa had gone to work as usual, and my sister, Willie, was with her fiancé. When Ma opened the door, we stared right into the barrel of a machine gun. A second soldier held a list which indicated the registration numbers of the guns each family possessed. I got our two weapons and handed them over without a word. People who were unable or unwilling to turn over their weapons were immediately dragged to the street and shot. We heard intermittent gunfire all evening. From our window I saw bloody bodies lying in the street where soldiers left them as a reminder that they meant business.

From here on out German officials added daily demands: curfew, blackout curtains, food and fuel rationing. Occupation officers ordered Dutch citizens to turn over all copper to them. Pa explained that copper could be melted and used in shells. One night some friends and I took all our copper and dumped it into the nearest canal.

With each demand came less freedom. Normally food filled our markets, but not enough to feed the entire German nation. All the country south of our apartment building was covered in greenhouses with fields and fruit orchards in between.

Within weeks, soldiers had raided most of the supplies from the stores. A symphony of train whistles reminded us of the carloads of food being transported to Germany. With the departing trains we realized that the Germans had invaded The Netherlands for her food supplies. Our country was expected to provide food for our enemies. Soon food was scarce at our table. Rationing became a fact of life.

Pa said that most shop owners had closed up and sold their remaining inventories at inflated prices on the Black Market. My father, who was owner and president of a bakery employing 1,000 workers, continued to produce at full capacity and sell whatever he produced. Later the Nazis caught many businessmen who had sold on the Black Market and sent them to camps in Germany. We heard a little bit about these German camps, but had no idea of the horrors that went on inside them.

It seemed that each day we received fewer rations. Before long children under ten got one egg a week and later only one egg a month. By this time most food items including sugar, flour, meat, coffee and tea were rationed. We became hungrier all the time.

In the greenhouses, farmers continued to grow vegetables, berries and grapes. As I bicycled down country roads south of our apartment building I saw German soldiers guarding the greenhouses and orchards to prevent theft by Dutch people. In fact, some of the guards were Dutch. For extra rations, Dutch men would patrol the fields for the Germans. I told my father how shocked I was that some people were willing to sell out their countrymen for a small price.

"This may be only the first of many shocks you'll experience, Son," my father commented.

Because I knew some of the farmers, they allowed me to sneak into their greenhouses to get food. Either late at night or early in the morning, I put on my raincoat, hopped on my bicycle and pedaled to a familiar greenhouse. I opened the door and pushed my bike inside. After stuffing vegetables inside the closed lining of my coat, I bicycled home, my raincoat billowing out over the carriage rack of my bicycle. The guards gave me some questioning looks, but fortunately I was never stopped. Although this food supplemented our rations my stomach rumbled almost constantly.

Within days of the occupation the Dutch people got tired of the bad treatment, and to get revenge, formed an underground. My father and I eagerly joined after being asked by friends. Our meeting place became the cemetery across the canal, west of our apartment house. Pa was made commander of a group, but we never worked together.

On every outing we risked our lives. One of my first times out, the underground decided to sabotage a warehouse where the Germans stored canned fruit and vegetables destined for Germany. Several guards had been posted around the building.

I was so angry at the Germans for the suffering they'd caused my family and countrymen that I forced my fear deep inside, never letting my fellow underground members know how afraid I felt. After dark, three underground members and I sneaked past one guard and hid in some bushes in the back of the building. Another underground member had scouted out the warehouse, so we already had a plan of action. We waited five or six minutes—it seemed like two days—for the opportunity to break in.

When no guards were in sight, we applied tape to a window completely covering it over. After tapping around the edges, we soundlessly lifted out the single unbroken piece of glass. Being the most slender, I crawled through the opening and unlatched the window for everyone else.

Once inside, we took ice picks and got revenge against our enemy by puncturing every can within reach. Because the boxes were not sealed we easily ruined the cache leaving no evidence. By early morning we'd done our damage and escaped. I've always wondered what would have happened if we'd been caught. Likely we would have been shot in our tracks. What I would have given to have seen the faces of the German soldiers on the eastern front when they opened the cans and discovered the food was spoiled.

Since I was a member of the underground, practically every day was a challenge. We never missed an opportunity to take out our frustrations on our enemy. Although we missed seeing the faces of German soldiers digging into cans of spoiled food, an opportunity soon came where we could see the angry faces of our thwarted enemy.

On a Saturday afternoon in July of 1940 several Sea Scouts and I biked to Kaag Lake. We'd gone to check on our two Sea Scout—a branch of the Boy Scouts—sailboats docked there. All of us had special feelings for these boats because we'd spent many hours earning money to buy them. I remembered fun times with my buddies learning to sail our boats, and then to swim and dive from them. When I was thirteen years old I'd won the world Sea Scout sailing competition using one of our boats. Of course sailing on our home lake gave me an advantage because I knew the winds, the shoreline and how to navigate the lake to my advantage.

On that warm Saturday afternoon, from the opposite shore, we saw our boats out on the lake. *What's going on?* I thought. Through binoculars I saw young men about my age, in brown Hitler Youth uniforms with a swastika on the left sleeve, trying to sail our boats. They had no idea how to handle them. One boat had capsized and they didn't know how to right it.

"If we can't sail our boats, they can't either," I mumbled to my friends. They agreed.

During the week we rigged up snorkeling gear. Each of us cut a hole through the center of a cork and forced it over the end of a two foot length of garden hose. With corks at the top, our breathing tubes would float. We piled up our make-shift snorkeling tubes, hand drills and camping gear in readiness.

The following Saturday evening we returned to Kaag Lake prepared to stop the Hitler Jugend. By sunset we could see from the opposite shore that the Hitler Youth had left for their evening activities. We slipped hand drills through our belts, slid into the lake and swam across underwater. We came up under our sailboats and began to drill. Before long we'd drilled so many holes that the boats began to sink. Quietly we swam back across the lake and camped overnight to wait for the discovery.

Seeing the shocked looks on the faces of the Hitler Youth the next morning was more than worth our efforts. Only the tips of the masts stood above the water. We were too far away to hear their comments, but through binoculars we could see the anger and frustration in their expressions and gestures. That was real satisfaction.

On another night during the first couple of months of the occupation, Jaap-a schoolmate-and I went into a cafeteria for dinner. Several German soldiers were already dining. As I went to hang my raincoat, I noticed a military raincoat with a belt and gun-in-holster hanging over it. This gave me an idea. My raincoat had an opening in the side of the pocket that allowed me to reach into the pocket of my trousers without opening my coat. I put my handkerchief in my coat pocket and hung my coat over the belt and holster. After taking a couple of steps away, I started to cough and sneeze. I patted my trouser pockets as if looking for my handkerchief. Not finding it, I walked back to the coat rack. I reached into my raincoat pocket, and through the opening took the gun from the holster and slipped it into my coat pocket. In a continuous motion, I slid out my handkerchief and blew my nose. Pretending I had to leave, I threw my raincoat over my arm and casually strolled out.

When I realized what a chance I'd taken, my heart thudded in my chest. I sprinted as fast as I could, splashing through alleys until I was out of that neighborhood. As I ran I wondered what Jaap and his father thought of gun registration now.

In 1938, when the gun registration law had been enacted, Jaap's father had lectured, "This law will reduce crime and make Holland a safer place to live." Most of the population had agreed, and being law abiding citizens dutifully registered their guns. I doubt if many people had anticipated two years earlier how easy that law would make it for the Germans to leave us defenseless.

I worried about Jaap, who was still in the cafeteria. Later he told me that when the German soldier missed his gun he stomped around, swore and shouted threats. He had the manager lock the door and while his buddy held a gun on everyone he searched all the patrons thoroughly, including women.

When I'd reached safety and had a chance to examine the gun, I saw it had a "W" engraved with a crown above it. That meant that the gun had been taken from the Dutch army.

I knew then that I had not stolen the gun, but had taken it back from a thief. When I got home I showed the gun to Pa. He recognized the type and took it with him to the underground. At least this gun would be used in defense of Dutchmen.

CHAPTER III

Enemies
Seen and Unseen

E VERY DAY LIFE BECAME DARKER and hunger became one more enemy. One evening my parents invited some good friends over for a bridge game. During the evening, Mr. Mooi had to pass by the kitchen to reach the bathroom. When he returned to the game he apologized, "I'm so ashamed, but I ate your last potato. How much do I owe you?" My parents refused payment, saying they were happy to share the extra potato.

As the occupation continued, not only food but fuel ran low. All but the rich rode streetcars or "Trams," buses and bicycles. Before long I noticed that more and more buses pulled a little trailer behind which carried a wood burner. When I asked Pa, he explained, "Engineers have adapted automobile engines to burn wood gas because the Germans have taken most of our oil and gas supplies. Now our enemies are forcing us to cut wood for fuel from our dwindling forests."

Another reason to hate the Germans, I thought. *They're stealing our resources to make war on us and our allies.*

Living through an occupation brings out the ingenuity in people. Early in the occupation my grandfather, Pa's father, owned a truck for his furniture moving business. When gas became scarce he removed the windshield, hooked up a team of horses and used his truck for a carriage.

Dutch people have always used bicycles for transportation, but during the war more than ever. When bicycle tires were no longer available we again used ingenuity. We'd take off our front wheel, extend the front end fork, and put on a solid rubber tire from a baby carriage. This way the good tire could be saved for use when a rear wheel wore out. You had to ride very carefully with these small hard rubber tires, as I found out the hard way. When I hit one tiny rock on the road I flipped flat onto the ground.

One afternoon when I was riding downtown on an errand for my mother, the German military roared in and turned their vehicles sideways to block off a couple of streets. Soldiers scurried around confiscating everything from bicycles to fur coats from everyone in the blocked-off area. A young German soldier grabbed my bike out from under me. As he had with the other bicycles, he jumped onto it to ride to the end of the block where a truck was parked to collect the "loot." I'd already converted the front wheel of my bike to a carriage wheel, but the others he'd collected had not been changed. The soldier took off down the street, hit a pebble and sprawled smack on his rear end. It was all I could do to keep from laughing out loud.

The soldier, his cheeks red with rage, got up and threw the bike at me. *Eine dumme esel.* "You dumb ass," he yelled.

After I got home I told Pa the story and he laughed so hard he almost fell off his chair. It was great to see because there wasn't much to laugh about these days.

As months went by, life became more unpredictable. Being a young man during an occupation wasn't much fun. I'd turned seventeen on the 17th of September, but there was nothing to celebrate and little to celebrate with. School routine became the only thing I could count on to stay the same.

I missed my friend Fred who had dropped out of school after his father died in the bombing of Rotterdam. I wished for the old

1938, Queen Wilhelmina's Fortieth Anniversary Parade. Jack dressed in seafarer costume.

days of going to the movies and playing sports with my friends, of sailing in Sea Scout regattas, of swimming in the North Sea until our skin turned so blue that not even a dare could get us back into the water.

I remembered the fun of celebrating Queen Wilhelmina's 40th anniversary in 1938. After the boys in my school had marched in the parade wearing historical costumes, all 200 of us were invited to a reception at the palace. The Queen, who had daughters only, must not have understood how boys act. After two hot hours of parading we were very thirsty. When servants passed out soft drinks in crystal glasses we quickly emptied them, hid them under tables draped with long white tablecloths and asked for more. A classmate accidentally kicked over some glasses under a table and they started crashing like crystal dominoes. Guards immediately asked us to leave. Would life ever be that much fun again?

Pa and I had a good laugh over the shattered crystal at the expense of Queen Wilhelmina. Ma and Willie didn't join in. Willie especially felt a strong loyalty for our Queen because she was named after her. When I'd finished my story, Pa reminded us of his one run in with the Queen's authority. One day before the war we'd been watching the Queen pass through the streets of The Hague in her carriage. Everyone was expected to show the Queen respect by coming to attention. Pa turned his back on her to demonstrate his anti-royalist sentiments. A police officer marched over to him and asked that he give our Queen the honor she deserved. He refused. The policeman hauled him off to jail to spend one night. He'd been angry at the time, but now we could chuckle over Pa's escapade. These humorous moments became more precious as the occupation stretched into a year. It was the spring of 1941.

Still there was no sign that our enemies would ever give us back our freedom. As the months passed each hour became more dangerous. Not only did we have to be careful of German soldiers, but we had to look out for Dutch people who collaborated with the enemy. A young man my age, who lived about a block away, joined the German army. When he came home after training he strutted through our neighborhood like he owned it. Later, when we heard that he had been killed on the Russian front, we celebrated. But many of our enemies were more secretive than he.

Pa's and my double life continued; businessman or student by day, worker in the underground at night. My father slipped out into the dark every night, and I nearly as often. He never talked about his missions and I never talked about mine. While on assignments we painted our faces black. No one was known by his real name. Even the names we were given were changed regularly, so that if interrogated, we couldn't reveal to our captors who the other underground members were.

Our enemies took complete control of every phase of our lives. By orders of the German occupation authorities, lights in our homes could not be turned on unless the windows were covered with heavy curtains. By the same token, headlights on all vehicles driven at night had to be covered with black paper. A narrow slit, like the eyes of a sleepy child, allowed just enough light to escape to illuminate the way. One night as I gazed out our living room window toward our city of The Hague, it looked as if the sea had swallowed up the land. All street lights had been turned off to make bombing raids difficult for the allies.

Those of us in the underground turned the pitch darkness and water engorged canals into allies. The German soldiers who patrolled the streets and canals at night didn't know the area making them vulnerable to accidents, planned or unplanned.

Because soldiers frequently fell into the canals, the Germans built fences to block them off. Big arrows were posted along the streets to direct the occupation forces across canal bridges and from town to town. We in the underground changed the arrows and removed the fences, sending many a truck driver or motorcycle messenger to death by drowning.

One dark night my underground group set a trap just down the road from our apartment complex. We didn't worry about catching a Dutch citizen, as all private vehicles had been confiscated long ago. Directly in front of our apartment building ran a street that dead-ended into a swift-moving stream south of us. A bridge crossed the canal north of us, so my underground group took the arrow that pointed across the bridge and turned it to face south down the dead-end street. We hid and watched as a motorcycle messenger followed the arrow, turned down our dead-end street and plunged straight into the stream at the end. We pounced onto him to make sure he was dead and took his possessions.

As I searched the soldier's pockets I thought, *I'm glad he's dead. He's taken our freedom, security, food and the lives of Dutch citizens. It's only fair that he should die.*

We threw his body back into the stream with his motorcycle. On our way home we turned the arrow to point back across the bridge.

Punishment followed immediately. Any time the underground succeeded in their missions the Germans would enforce an earlier curfew in a limited area, as in this case, or all over for more wide spread infractions. Instead of the usual 10:00 P.M. to 5:00 A.M.

curfew, we were now forced to observe a 6:00 to 5:00 curfew. That didn't eliminate our underground work; it just made it more challenging.

One of our bigger challenges came the night when we attempted to off-set train tracks on a trestle going over a river. The train trestle crossed over the river separate from the bridge that carried cars, bicycles, and pedestrians. Unlike the traffic bridge it had no railing. That night several underground members and I carried crow bars under our raincoats to the site of our mission. As unobtrusively as possible we pulled out the spikes at the front end of the bridge, then pried the tracks over bracing the weight of our bodies against the crow bars. We grunted, groaned, swore and sweated for twenty minutes to get that track to move just an inch. Then we found a hiding place behind some trees along the river. We waited and watched impatiently to see what kind of damage our handy work would cause.

Just before sunrise we heard a train coming. The engine hit the off-set tracks and leaped over the side of the trestle. That was one big splash! The engine was traveling so fast that it pulled most of the freight cars into the river after it. *Here's one train load of food that won't reach the German soldiers on the eastern front,* I thought jubilantly.

It seemed the Nazis tried to control even our friendships. Right after the occupation, a "no meetings" rule was established. A group of more that three people was considered a meeting. The no meetings rule did not apply to the National Socialist Beweging or Movement, or N.S.B.'ers as they were known in Dutch. From the beginning of the occupation these traitors declared their loyalty to the Germans and worked for the benefit of the Germans. In the minds of many Dutch people this group was made up of "lazy bums," those who would take advantage of any situation. They courted favors from our enemies, schemed for more food and spied on their fellow citizens. Their distinctive black uniforms, with black-and-red arm bands printed with swastikas, made them easy to spot. One of their tasks was to help the enemy patrol the streets. When downtown we'd see them showing off their strength in groups of local members or by marching with N.S.B.'ers from other towns. In the parade they'd proudly carry their flags of red and black horizontal stripes. The loyal Dutch said, "Their flag represents what they are, red on the outside and black on the inside."

Several of these *quislings* lived in our neighborhood. As I biked to school I noticed many of their apartment windows had been smashed out by rocks. An ice cream parlor a few blocks from our apartment, owned by a man whose son was a quisling, rarely had any whole windows, in part because of my good marksmanship.

Friends told of incidents when quislings happily betrayed their countrymen, and these traitors especially relished turning in a Jewish family found in hiding. After the Gestapo picked up the Jewish family, the quislings would be allowed to ransack the Jewish home as a reward for their loyalty. I wondered, *Are Sammy Cohen and his family all right?* I worried because I hadn't seen Sammy, a boyhood friend, for several years and didn't know how to contact him. I missed getting together with Sammy and his family to celebrate Jewish holidays.

At least the N.S.B.'ers were visible and more easily avoided. It was the plain-clothed Dutch traitors who were more dangerous. As it turned out, one of these—Rieta—lived on the same floor as my family.

Rieta was the daughter of a retired Army officer and his wife. Before the occupation Rieta had married a Navy man. When her husband left for England with the Dutch Navy, she gave up her apartment and moved in with her parents. Not long after the occupation Rieta started dating German soldiers.

The first night I came home from an underground mission and heard Rieta and a man on the staircase, I ducked behind the stairs and hid until the German soldier left. When I told my parents what I'd witnessed and overheard, Ma said, "I've already seen her during the daytime out walking with a German soldier. I wonder what

Rieta's parents think about her carrying on?" Looking at me with concern, she added, "Now you be extra careful, Ko." Ko was my nickname from Jacobus.

From then on we avoided the family next door as much as possible. Not knowing when the German soldier would appear doubled the risk Pa and I took in our underground activities. We made sure we left the house before the soldier arrived and came home after he left, unless the curfew had changed again.

The fluctuation in the curfew and the irregular schedule of Rieta's German soldier boyfriend made it tricky to leave and get home safely. I usually returned from my underground assignments by running through dark streets and alleys. If I heard a German or N.S.B.'er vehicle I would hide in stairways or bushes. Now upon reaching home, I had to double- and triple-check to see if Rieta and her *Rot mof*, or "rotten German," were making out on the stairway.

Early in the occupation, the road west of the beach town of Scheveningen, where my school was located, had been blocked off to keep Dutch people from crossing the one hundred miles of the North Sea to England. Before the blockade several groups had boated across safely. On my daily trips to school I watched the progress of the Germans as they built a fifty-mile-long wall along the coast and painted it in camouflage colors. One of my jobs in the underground was to take pictures of the wall and the installations near it. Guards continually patrolled the area. I always carried my student permit, so I moved around without causing much suspicion. I used a box camera and holding it waist high behind my trusty raincoat took rolls of pictures. The same evening I delivered the rolls I'd taken that day to an underground member at our meeting place in the cemetery.

One night I took the undeveloped film to our meeting spot behind an old tombstone where Jan sat waiting in the drizzle. Unexpectedly a truck stopped at the entrance. We heard the clatter of guns as soldiers jumped off the truck. A shot and a ping rang out. I guessed that they'd shot the lock off the gate. Then I heard the footsteps of soldiers running between gravestones.

Fear tore at my gut. "This is the end," I whispered. Some bastard had betrayed us. We'd never been disturbed here before.

"No use running," Jan said. "That's a good way to get killed." He gripped the film in his raincoat pocket. "I'm sure they'll search the whole damned cemetery. There's just one way to solve this." He let out a long ghoulish howl.

To my surprise the soldiers turned tail and ran. I never would have believed it if I hadn't seen it. Those heroes of the Third Reich were such cowards.

First betrayal!

CHAPTER IV

Betrayal

I T WAS 1942, AND AFTER two years of occupation everything looked hopeless. Food was scarce and the Black Market could no longer supply enough merchandise. Pa managed to smuggle some bread home from his factory. But even that had become difficult, because several of his 1000 employees were German sympathizers and he didn't know who they were.

All food was rationed by this time. I continued to smuggle vegetables from the greenhouses and in good weather hid them in the bow and stern of a canoe. A friend and I paddled down the canals as if on a holiday and for some reason the soldiers left us alone.

That winter my family ran out of heating coal. None was available at any price. Wood fences dividing the small yards on the first floor level had already been torn down and burned. One morning as I biked across the bridge north of our apartment, I noticed that a couple of brick sized blocks of wood, making up the masonry-like surface of the bridge, had been removed. By the next morning the whole top layer of wood blocks had disappeared. In our desperation for fuel we and others were willing to burn creosote soaked wood to keep a single room of our apartments warm.

Despite betrayers, during the first two years of the occupation Pa and I managed to hold on to our ham radio. Through it we received news of the war from England and passed this news on to our friends and members of the underground. We'd also made a simple transmitter to send news of the German occupation to Eng-

land. Then the Germans set up jammers along the coast, and the
only broadcasts we could pick up were filled with German propaganda. We sifted this information from what we knew to be the real
facts and passed it on.

To foil the jammers and get uncensored news once again, Pa and
I made a special antenna—a cross with wires spun over it on a
swivel base. By turning this homemade device, we were able to
again receive a clear voice from England. Every evening at 6:00, we
took the antenna outside and set it up on our balcony at the rear of
our apartment to listen to the news. Immediately afterward we hid
the antenna back in the closet. We had to be careful who we shared
the news with.

By July of 1942, twenty-five students and I had finished the
requirements to graduate in the study of aerodynamics from The
Netherlands Aircraft Institute. A date for the ceremony was set, and
we were told to bring a lunch. The closer the graduation date drew,
the more nervous I became. One other student and I acted on our
suspicions and stayed home. Later that day we heard that the Germans, desperate for anyone with a technical degree, had loaded the
graduates aboard a bus and transported them to Germany, never to
be seen again.

Second betrayal, I thought. *Thank God, I've dodged the Germans
again.*

Without a student permit, I could now be arrested at any time.
I took up the habit of wearing baggy cloths and of walking with a
limp when around German authorities.

My friend, Jaap, told me about some of his relatives who lived on
a farm in Groningen in the northern part of The Netherlands. He
suggested I hide there and gave me directions. I rode my bike to the
farm, staying on secondary roads. My good sense of direction and
biking experiences during vacations with friends throughout Europe,
stood me in good stead. Jaap's family took me in, but for only ten days.

"Having you here puts you and us in great danger from the
'Landwacht'," said Jaap's uncle. "They're a quisling group that

checks the farms for illegal workers. If you were caught you'd be sent to factories in Germany, the same ones being bombed by the British and Americans." Jaap's relatives didn't say how they'd be punished, but I could guess.

I didn't have another choice so I pedaled back home. My family and friends were surprised to see me after only two weeks. They'd thought I would be gone for the remainder of the occupation.

I rejoined the underground and soon learned that the other student who'd skipped out on graduation had disappeared. Years later I found out that he was killed when the Dutch and American Armies recaptured Holland. I began to feel as if a betrayer lurked around every corner. It became even more important than ever to avoid Rieta's German soldier boyfriend.

In late August of 1942 our doorbell rang. My whole family was home. I hid in a walk-in closet next to the front door, as had become my practice. My mother, whose arthritis had flared up, walked stiffly to open the door.

I heard Rieta's voice. "Good evening, Mrs. van der Geest."

Without inviting Rieta in, my mother asked, "What can I do for you?"

"Is your daughter, Willie, home?"

"Yes," answered my mother and called Willie.

My sister came to the door and Rieta asked, "What are you doing tomorrow night?"

"I have a date with my fiancé."

Rieta ignored my sister's answer. "I have a blind date set up for you."

"I don't want a blind date even if he could see," quipped Willie.

Rieta cut her off. "You'd better be home at 6:30 tomorrow night if you know what's good for you." I heard her footsteps as she turned and walked across the landing to her parents' apartment.

I came out of the closet in time to hear my mother comforting Willie. "We'll work it out, dear."

"I don't want any of you to get hurt," Willie said. My family spent the rest of that evening discussing what should be done.

Finally my mother said, "Willie, you leave and see Koo as planned. I'll handle this situation."

The next day was tension filled, inside and outside of our apartment. That evening Willie, after returning from her secretarial job, left with her fiancé before Pa had arrived home from work. Ma answered the door and faced Rieta and her soldier friends alone.

I could see Rieta and the German soldiers through a small window in my hiding place in the closet overlooking the landing.

Ma invited them in and began her acting career.

"It's not that you are German," she explained pleasantly to Willie's date, "but it isn't right for my daughter to have a date when she's engaged to be married. I'm sure you agree."

They talked for several more minutes, and the officer left, politely saying, "Auf Wiedersehen."

My mother's chance encounter with the German soldier was to prove fortuitous for her when they met again less than a year later. He demonstrated that all German soldiers were not brutes.

The next week I ran into Rieta on the staircase.

"You must quit sending messages to England," she hissed. "I've heard you."

I knew Rieta's family didn't have a receiver, so she must have heard our transmissions on her regular radio. Our signal must have bled into their radio signal because she was so close to the transmitter.

As I stood listening, every threatening word Rieta spoke stung like a whip lash to my body. She was already angry that Willie had refused to go out on the blind date she'd arranged. Now she knew about our transmissions. Did she also suspect my father and I were in the underground?

At that moment I wished the underground had done to her what we'd done to other Dutch women who'd dated German soldiers. She deserved to have all her hair cut off to show that she'd been a traitor to her people. But I hadn't dared suggest it for fear that she would recognize me or my voice and turn me in.

Within hours the Gestapo came and took all of our ham radio equipment; transmitter, receiver and antenna. For several weeks afterward we felt extremely apprehensive.

In September Willie got married and she and Koo moved in with his parents.

Three evenings later my parents and I heard insistent banging on our front door.

"Is that Willie and Koo?" my mother asked in alarm, rising from the dinner table to answer the door. We'd just been talking about them. Pa and I followed.

Two German soldiers stood with machine guns and a civilian with a hand gun pointed at us.

"You're coming with us," said the officer in charge.

I felt sick to my stomach. There was no escape. I'd already seen many examples of German brutality, and there was no reason to believe we'd be spared.

While one of the soldiers kept his gun aimed at us, the other two went through the house and gathered my father's typewriter, copy machine and the radio from our living room. Pa and I were forced to carry the equipment downstairs to a waiting truck.

About halfway down the stairs I met Rieta.

She flashed her brilliant smile, and said, "This is my revenge."

I hated her. It was all I could do to keep from throwing the typewriter into her grinning face. How could she do this to fellow Dutchmen?

Betrayal number three!

CHAPTER V

Prisoners

I SILENTLY WATCHED MY PARENTS as the soldiers drove us downtown in the bed of an open truck. Ma's face turned pale and she grimaced as each bounce battered her arthritic body. Pa held her gnarled hand, his slender face drawn in worry. The truck stopped in front of a government building that had been taken over by the Germans. Two guards at the door stared as the Gestapo herded us through the entrance. The soldiers threw our typewriter, copy machine and radio on a desk, and filled out some papers. They then drove us to a prison in the beach town of Scheveningen where my former school was located. The building that was now the prison had been known as the Orange Hotel, after the House of Orange of the ruling family of The Netherlands. Guards carrying guns and whips escorted us into the prison hallway.

"Stand with your noses against the wall," barked a guard. "Take two steps back and hold your hands behind your backs."

In this awkward position most of our weight rested on our noses. I looked out of the corner of my eye and saw Ma's knees buckle. I quickly walked over and picked up a folding metal chair for her. A guard saw me, yanked the chair from my hands and whacked me across the back with it. The blow knocked me to the floor, sucking the wind completely out of me. I couldn't move for a minute. When I looked up another guard was dragging Pa toward an office.

They're just going to question him, then bring him back, I thought. That was the last time I ever saw my father.

33

I watched as they took my mother away. Tears rolled down her cheeks. I wanted to go to her, but the guard standing above me held his whip over his shoulder ready to attack. Ma turned and our eyes met briefly. Little did I know that it would be many years before I would see her again.

With Ma out of sight, the chair-wielding guard grabbed my arm, pulled me to my feet, dragged me to a cell and threw me inside. Alone now, I sat down on the filthy cot, dropped my head into my shaking hands to think over what had happened. I was in a daze. It was crazy. Ma and Pa had been taken away and I could think only one thought. *Our old fox terrier, Jony, was left behind. Had the apartment door been left open? Who would feed and water her?*

As I sat in confusion I heard a muffled tapping sound. I held my breath and didn't move. There it was again. My cell was one of several in a row, but the cells on either side of me were empty.

That's Morse code, I thought. Then I made out the question, "Who-are-you?"

I'd learned Morse code at fourteen when Pa taught me how to use a ham radio. I pounded out my name. The prisoner answered, and in his excitement or inexperience his message came through garbled. I tapped for him to repeat.

"Where-are-you-from?" he pounded out carefully. Soon another prisoner joined in the questioning. After a couple of hours we'd learned each others names, home towns, about our families and why we were being held. In my isolation and misery I felt comforted by these contacts. Late that night the prison grew quiet.

Still I could not sleep thinking about all that had happened to my family in the past twelve hours. As I tossed and turned on the narrow cot, I relived our arrest over and over again. Ma's health was a great concern to me. For years she'd suffered from crippling arthritis, causing her fingers to curl and become useless for many tasks. Medication helped to relieve her pain, but I was sure the pills had been left behind in the rush to get us to prison. Pa, although healthy, had a slight build and no longer had the strength of a young man. I thought of my sister, Willie, and brother-in-law, Koo. I hoped they had not been arrested for our "political crimes."

Early the next morning, a guard opened the cell door and commanded me to carry the barrel that served as a toilet out and down the hall. A carpet runner ran along the middle of the hallway. I didn't realize that prisoners weren't allowed to walk on the runner. A guard's swift kick to my ankle with his combat boot and a profanity-filled order quickly taught me this rule. I stumbled down the hall, almost dropping my load. At the end of the hall, stationed behind sandbags, a German soldier crouched with a gun pointed at the prisoners coming to empty their barrels. I followed the line outside and around the corner to what looked like a swimming pool. The stench told me it had to be a cesspool. At first I thought I was supposed to empty my own barrel. Then I saw two Jews standing chest deep in the excrement-filled pool taking our barrels to empty them.

Guards nudged each other, making crude jokes and laughing at the Jews. I thought those bastards had warped senses of humor. *How could they be so cruel?*

An hour after I'd been taken back to my cell, the guard returned. Through a little opening in the door he handed me a tin cup filled with a warm brown liquid, what they called coffee. I drank it greedily, though in no way did it resemble coffee in looks or flavor. At this point I still thought my father, mother and I would be interviewed and released.

It was not long before the door opened again and a guard motioned me into the hall. Several other prisoners waited there. I wondered if any of them had tapped out messages to me in Morse code the night before, but didn't dare ask. The guards had ordered us to be silent. We were herded together and marched out into a courtyard. I looked around for Ma and Pa, but saw neither one. Still I felt hopeful. This truck might take us downtown for interviews and my parents would be there.

I soon found out how many men could be crammed into the bed of a truck. After we'd been loaded, soldiers threw a tarp over us so that people we passed wouldn't know what kind of cargo the truck carried. The other prisoners and I had no idea where we were being driven, though I sensed we had headed east back toward The Hague. It quickly became evident that the trip would not be a short one. As the military truck jounced and rattled down the road, I became more and more anxious about my parents. All I could do was hope that we were being transported to the same place.

Late that afternoon the truck stopped in Vught, a small town south of s'Hertogenbosch, where a good sized concentration camp was located. Still we'd been given no food or drink. During our trip they'd "forgotten" to give us anything, a soldier told us.

We climbed down from the truck and, along with many other newly arrived prisoners, were marched into a building to have our heads shaved. "This will prevent the spread of lice," we were informed. Soldiers handed out pants and shirts of thin gray material, with no thought to sizing. All our personal clothing and anything contained in the pockets disappeared. Now I felt like an official prisoner, drab and dispirited. With a sinking feeling, hope of meeting up with my parents faded.

That evening all of us prisoners were loaded into boxcars and cattle cars. I felt lucky to be in a cattle car where some ventilation came through the slats. We'd been packed in like pickles in a jar. Some older men who couldn't climb the steep steps were taken a short distance away and shot. With each burst of gunfire I twitched and felt the bodies around me do the same.

The guards' message became clear. "We don't tolerate any feeble people around here."

This is for real, I thought. The guards' actions left no doubt in my mind that the Nazis were not playing around. I worried about Ma and Pa and wondered if they, especially my mother, could climb such steep stairs. Or would another young man or woman on another train watch them get shot and wonder whose parents they were.

When the guards had finished loading the prisoners, and we'd heard the last door clang shut, the train sat for a long time. The sun set. Exhaustion overcame me and I dozed on my feet. Finally the train jolted into action. When it got to full speed, the cold September air blew through the slats, but we'd been squeezed in so tightly that our body heat kept each other warm. Occasionally the train made short stops. The stops lasted only long enough to add more prisoner-filled cars or to remove dead bodies and replace them with fresh ones. In weariness some of us tried to sit down. There was no room. In the darkness a light rain began to fall. Everyone wished the rain would fall harder as none of us had had a drink in many hours. Some prisoners tried to push to the side to reach through the slats and collect enough rain water to moisten their mouths. My mouth had gotten so dry that I had trouble swallowing, but I was so closed in I couldn't move toward the rain. The rain didn't last long enough to do anyone much good.

The train kept moving through the night. Even with the wind blowing through our cattle car, the smell of human urine and excrement got worse by the hour. We'd never been allowed to use the bathroom at any stop. It got to the point where I could hold it no longer. Though I felt embarrassed, I had to urinate on myself.

Everyone kept to himself. Again I thought about Ma and Pa and even our dog. *Would my parents be able to hold up under the harsh conditions I had already experienced? Is there any way to get out of this mess?* I knew there was little chance of escape, let alone of finding my parents.

It was a living nightmare. I could still picture Rieta standing on the stairway with that damnable smile on her face, saying, "This is my revenge."

I hope she gets punished in triplicate. No one should get away with what she's done.

The train moved on at an even pace. This familiar rhythm took me back to an earlier train ride I'd made when I was not quite six years old. My grandfather, Ma's father, who'd driven a Tram for the city of The Hague, sometimes gave me free rides. One day I got off the tram near the train station without telling Grandfather. I jumped a fence to reach a train platform. There sat the train to Rotterdam, where we'd said good-bye to relatives many times before. I got aboard, thinking I'd stop by for a surprise visit. The sound of the whistle excited me, and I settled down to enjoy the twenty to thirty minute ride. The train never stopped in Rotterdam. As it turned out, I had boarded The Hague-to-Paris express. In Paris I got off, and without feeling afraid, I wandered the streets of Paris until dark. A French gendarme stopped and asked, "Are you lost?" He took me to the police station and contacted my parents. Pa came and got me. For the next few days it was very difficult to sit. Even so this first taste of travel only made me want to see more of the world.

The rank odors and cramped conditions in the cattle car brought me back to this hellish ride. When the train stopped again, we could hear German soldiers yelling orders at each other and at the train station workers. The German language is harsh and guttural. I had learned German as well as French and English at school. So I figured that we were now in Germany.

Our journey continued and we rolled through blacked out railroad stations. As in The Netherlands, windows of houses and headlights of vehicles were covered.

All of a sudden the train stopped. The mass of bodies in our car surged forward. It felt like there was more room in the car. The only way I could explain this was that we'd all lost weight. Days had passed, and we had still not been given a bit of food or water. Several bodies lay on the floor, either passed out or dead. We'd barely regained our balance from the sudden stop when I heard the rattle of gunfire. Everyone froze in place. Silence. Suddenly more bursts of gunfire.

"Somebody tried to escape," said a man next to me.

"God, I hope he succeeded," I said to myself.

Our stop here grew long. Because of earlier night escape attempts, a spotlight now moved back and forth across the boxcars. After a while I heard more gunfire. It was morning by this time, but the sun hid behind dreary gray clouds. My mood was more dreary than the day. My God, to be treated worse than animals. I didn't know anyone who would treat their pets or farm animals this way.

Finally we got underway. Daylight or dark, it made little difference in our journey. Except that in daylight when the train curved to the left, we could see some closed boxcars with German soldiers riding on top. The lack of air inside those cars must have made them a living hell. I could imagine the people inside screaming and pounding against the walls.

Even though I hadn't had anything to drink, my bladder was full again. With no prospects of a bathroom stop I had no choice but to let it go as everyone else had done. The morning went very slowly. I tried to guess what time it was, but I had totally lost track.

After many hours, or so it seemed, soldiers unlocked our cattle car and ordered everyone off. Even at my age—nineteen that month—I could hardly get my legs to move after what must have been at least three days and two nights of standing. Some of the older men fell down. I stepped over the dead and dying on my way to the door and tried not to look at their faces.

As soldiers assembled us outside, I curiously watched other troops open the doors of the closed-in boxcars. No one came out. The troops pulled out bodies and threw them into a truck. I couldn't see if the prisoners were unconscious or dead, but they were all treated as if they were dead.

One of the men from my car asked a guard, "Could I have a drink of water?"

Before we knew it, a guard pulled a fire hose from the station wall and turned it full blast on us. Most of us were swept from our feet. We struggled to get up to the loud laughter of German soldiers. I could still see their smirking faces as they loaded us onto trucks headed for Buchenwald.

Trip from The Hague to Buchenwald in Weimar, Germany

CHAPTER VI

Buchenwald

O N THE SHORT TRUCK RIDE from the railroad spur leading to Buchenwald and the main gate, I scanned the huge camp surrounded by a charged barbed wire fence. Every thirty-five feet stood a guard tower, a machine gun barrel sticking out from its platform. As if guard towers and barbed wire fences weren't enough to discourage flight, a large searchlight attached to each tower erased the possibility of a night escape. Outside the camp a thick beech tree forest covered the hilly area. It must have been a beautiful spot once.

The truck stopped in front of a building next to the main guardhouse.

Raus, Schweinehunde! shouted an SS guard. "Out, you dirty pigdogs!"

Guards herded us off the truck and into lines, hitting and smacking our bodies with clubs and sticks. As we marched through the fortress-like entrance gate, I noticed the inscriptions molded in wrought iron: RECHT ODER UNRECHT MEIN VATERLAND! RIGHT OR WRONG, MY COUNTRY! And, ARBEIT MACHT FREI! WORK MAKES YOU FREE! Both axioms remain burned into my memory.

After we'd passed through the gate, a welcoming committee, made up of German shepherd dogs and club-swinging SS guards and mercenaries, lined the way forcing us to run toward the receiving building. Panic stricken, I used my six-foot-two, 185-pound body to force my way into the middle of the mass of men where I managed to avoid all but glancing blows to my back and arm. Snarling dogs snapped at the heels of prisoners running on the outside, causing them to yell, fall and be trampled by the crazed, screaming mob. I couldn't believe the inhumanity I saw. Guards shouted challenges, making a competition out of seeing who could knock down the most prisoners. They laughed uproariously as the weaker prisoners fell. I kept on running.

Once inside a cement block building, a room without windows or an exit, the door slammed behind us and we were left alone. There we stood, panting and sweating in the bright lights, as if caught under a searchlight. Tables lined one wall and a trough with faucets lined the opposite wall. Many men dashed for the faucets.

"Watch it!" an older man yelled. "Make sure water comes out, and not gas."

One fellow gingerly opened a faucet. "It's water!"

A stampede started for drinking and washing water. After we'd cleaned up, some of us lay down on the tables, others on the floor. Although I felt exhausted, the bright lights and my aching muscles made it difficult to sleep. I finally fell asleep, but for only a short while. The clanging of the door woke me.

SS officers ordered us up and out of the building. Groggily we staggered to our feet and into line. We were marched to Barracks X, the bath and disinfectant building according to the sign. Guards commanded us to undress and barbers gave us another haircut. My barber started by placing clippers on my forehead and running them to the base of my neck. Five strokes and the job was done. Most of us were still bald from our haircut at the first camp. This time the haircut didn't stop with our heads. With dull clippers, underarm, genital and anal hair were also removed, leaving us nicked and bleeding. From here we were led to a pool filled with creosote and ordered to get in.

I groaned with pain, every nick and cut stung like hell. I didn't want to submerge my head, but a smack on my crown by a Kapo convinced me I'd better duck under. We soon learned that Kapos were just glorified prisoners who for extra rations and privileges ran our barracks. Many of them had been criminals before they'd been sent to Buchenwald. The Nazis allowed them free reign to punish us any way they wished.

Without allowing us to rinse off, guards lined us up and handed out our official prison uniforms—striped black and white pants and shirt, and wooden clogs. The material's thinness told me that my uniform had been reused several times. From this point on I was no longer Jacobus van der Geest, but #512601, the number stamped on my shirt pocket.

Sewn under my number was a red triangle. The color indicated I was a political prisoner. Jehovah Witnesses and gays had purple triangles, and black marketeers were tagged with black triangles. Of course Jews wore yellow stars, as they'd been forced to do publicly for quite a while.

For a moment I smiled as I watched the prisoners who'd never worn clogs try to march to our block. Their clumsy efforts gave us one of the only amusing incidents we would experience in months.

In the distance, over the tops of dozens of barracks, I noticed what to me looked like a chapel. I thought, *Is that for the use of the inmates or the Germans?* Ironically, I soon learned it was for both. "That's the crematorium," a fellow prisoner informed me. A nauseating, sweetish-smelling smoke blowing our way from the chimney corrected my naive notion.

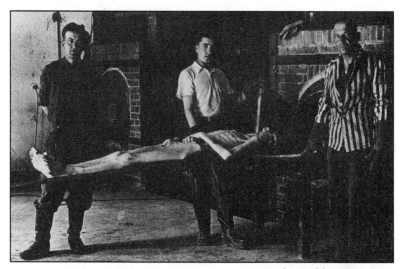

Buchenwald crematorium.

I'd just entered our home block when an inmate came over and tapped my shoulder. He'd obviously been in camp a long time, as his eyes were sunken into his skeletal face and he looked as if he weighed less than one hundred pounds.

"Jacobus?" he asked hoarsely.

I didn't recognize him.

"Jacobus," he repeated, "I'm Sammy's father."

"Oh, no," I said in shock. I compared how Mr. Cohen looked now to how he'd looked when I'd known him and his family in The Hague when Sammy and I were young boys.

"Where is Sammy?" I asked.

Tears rolled down Mr. Cohen's cheeks. "They killed him last week," he sobbed.

I put my hand on his arm. "Where is your wife?" I asked, tears coming to my eyes.

"I don't know. We were separated in Holland."

A Kapo ran over, grabbed Mr. Cohen, pushed him outside and clubbed him repeatedly, yelling, "You know you're forbidden to talk to Gentiles."

I stood immobilized by the scene of the skeletal old Mr. Cohen being beaten and the news he'd given me about Sammy's death.

Before I'd had time to comprehend what was going on, other prisoners and I were put on a clean-up kommando and ordered to scrub the barracks. I obeyed like a marionette. At least the task allowed me time to think about Sammy. Sammy was one of the few Jewish boys I'd known. I remember many times being invited to the Cohens' warm home behind their grocery store to share in Jewish holiday traditions and to eat the special foods served on those occasions. The Cohens were such a nice family. I couldn't understand the Germans' fanatic hatred of Jews. Until now, I'd never appreciated the freedom of religion we'd taken for granted in The Netherlands. Ma was Catholic, Pa was Lutheran, Jaap and his family Dutch Reformed, and the Cohens Jewish. I saw no conflict with our differences.

I swore to myself then and there that I would get out of this hell hole before I'd lost the weight that Sammy's father had.

Later our commandant assembled us for his welcoming speech.

"I'm your God now," he shouted. "I decide if you live or die. Remember that. Don't forget your numbers either. That's who you are."

Demonstrating his power, he thumped the nearest prisoner with a club. We all recoiled instinctively.

"Any disobedience will be punished by death," he bellowed.

His message came home strong and clear. Before such ruthlessness, my knees went weak and a feeling of helplessness crept through my entire body.

New prisoners were then turned loose to find an unoccupied sleeping space on one of the many platforms and to mark it with a blanket. Two layers of sleeping platforms lined each wall; the lower, one foot off the cement floor, the upper, four feet above the floor. Fifteen prisoners shared a platform. My survival instincts took over, and I pushed and shoved to grab a spot on the top layer. From the stench in the air and stains on the floor, it was obvious to me that some men couldn't or wouldn't go outside to use the latrine at night. I'd be damned if I'd sleep under them.

That evening the prisoners from my barracks marched, along with the many thousands of prisoners at Buchenwald, to the Appelplatz. In this large open area roll call was held every morning and evening. I learned later that Buchenwald had been built 1937 to house 10,000 prisoners. At it's peak it held 20,000 prisoners. It seemed that at least 20,000 names were called off at every roll call.

Each prisoner's number was shouted out, and if a prisoner did not answer, roll call was held up until that prisoner had been accounted for. Several men called out the prisoners names from different locations. It took from five to six hours of standing quietly at attention for this task to be completed. I felt I would die on my feet. A tin can of brown water, supposedly coffee, was all I'd had that day. On this late September evening, I focused my eyes on one of the last patches of green grass. I had to concentrate on this living thing, because my chances of surviving or escaping looked dim.

A lunch of potato-peeling soup followed roll call. If you were lucky, the soup actually had a peeling floating in it. After lunch all prisoners went to their work detail—from 11:30 until 5:00. In my first months I worked on a clean-up crew. In the evening it was back to the Appelplatz for roll call. Finally in shifts, prisoners from each barracks marched to a mess hall where we stood in line for a chunk of black bread. This was our ration for the day. Gnawing hunger became a way of life. The rations we'd been allotted at home seemed like a feast in comparison. And there would be no greenhouses from which to take more.

Early the next morning we faced roll call again. During the night several prisoners had died. Other prisoners, some who could barely get up themselves, dragged dead bodies out of the block and to roll call. Being young and still relatively strong, I lifted a body over my shoulder and started for the Appelplatz. A Kapo near the door hit me on the back with a club and shouted, *Schnell,* "Hurry." I lost my balance but recovered in time to make it to roll call.

Once in line I was not allowed to lay the body down until roll call ended. Even though the man weighed less than ninety pounds, holding him on my shoulder for more than five hours exhausted me. Finally I laid him on the ground, saying, *Er ist tot,* "He is dead." A guard laughed at my obvious statement. My back ached for two days.

The ache in my back was mild compared to what I saw other prisoners going through. One old Jew could hardly see. A Kapo had slapped him in the face knocking his glasses to the ground. Sadistically the brute stepped on the Jew's glasses, grinding them into the red dust. "Where's your God now," he yelled, "on vacation?"

I wondered the same myself. How could a caring God allow the cruelties I saw every day?

The uniforms we'd been issued the first day could not keep out the coolness of autumn. I saw the Germans' refusal to give us jackets as just another form of the power that the Kapos and SS guards never let up showing us. They considered any treatment fair. They'd taken away my identity, strength, dignity and pride, but not my will to live. Even so, every day became harder to bear as I lost more and more weight.

Every minute detail of our wretched lives came under SS control. Even going to the latrine was regimented. All prisoners' bowel movements were expected to conform to a Nazi schedule. After getting up, prisoners marched to the latrine located to one side of our barracks. It consisted of a wooden structure built over a long narrow ditch. It had no front or back, just two befouled six-by-six planks over the worm-and-fly-infested refuse. This indignity and all the other injustices made me want to kill every damned SS guard and Kapo in Buchenwald!

One spot in camp gave me solace and a little peace; a solitary tree where I'd heard that Goethe had sat for many hours thinking and writing poetry and plays. I doubt he ever anticipated all the horror that would take place around his thinking tree. It seemed a mockery to me that the tree had been left in remembrance of him.

Cool fall weather gave way to cold rains. Dust turned to mud. With each step we sank to our ankles in the bog and weaker prisoners fell. After work detail, guards ordered all muddy prisoners to strip outside before entering the barracks. Kapos ruled that no mud would be allowed in the buildings. Yet once inside we put back on the same foul prison uniforms and muddy clogs that we wore all the time. These masters of cruelty had found yet another way to weaken our bodies and spirits. What an irony not to allow mud into the buildings, when all prisoners were infested with lice and lived in abysmal filth because no provisions had been made for washing up.

During roll call a couple of days later I stood beside a young Jew about my age. Nazi soldiers paced around keeping order, habitual smirks on their faces. I watched as one of them finished his cigarette. I'd learned the value of a cigarette butt. Some prisoners craved tobacco over a hunk of bread. When the guard threw down the butt I'd planned to cover it with my clog until I could pick it up later.

Instead of flicking the butt to the ground, the SS guard strode over to the young Jewish man standing beside me and put the cigarette out on his cheek.

The Jew wailed in agony and fell to the ground.

God. Are you on vacation? my mind screamed, remembering the question asked by the Kapo. In the split second it took to think this thought, my Dutch temper flared. I kicked that SS bastard in the groin with all my strength. He doubled over clutching his crotch.

Guards rushed over and beat me on the head with rifles until my mind went black.

CHAPTER VII

The Hole

O
H MY GOD, I'M BLIND!" I called out, rubbing my eyes. My heart pounded so hard I could hardly breathe. "They've experimented on me and made me blind." My eyes felt normal, but I'd heard of other prisoners who'd been used for experiments, so nothing would surprise me.

I frantically groped around in the dark and discovered I'd been locked into a small cement cell—too low to stand in and too short to stretch out in. Slowly my reasoning came back, and I decided I wasn't blind after all. It was night.

My head hurt like hell. I rubbed a big bump there. A flashback, of the guard burning the young Jewish man on the cheek with his cigarette butt and of my beating, flooded back. "Oh, God," I whispered. What was I doing lying here bruised and filthy, crawling with bugs and calling upon God? I wondered angrily if God really did exist. In my mind a just God would never have allowed a harmless young Jew to be burned in the face with a cigarette butt. And what about all the other cruel tortures I'd seen? Would He have allowed those?

I lay in the darkness cursing God and trying to figure out where the hell I was and how long I'd been there. I ran my swollen tongue over the inside of my mouth. It felt dry as dust. My stomach seemed to be digesting itself. Despite the lack of food and water I still had to urinate. Desperate for something to drink, I had no choice but to lick the floor where I'd urinated. Soon I discovered that by urinating on the wall, I could more easily reach the liquid and while licking it take in a few cement particles to chew on to ease the burning in my stomach.

Many silent hours passed. With the solitude, memories and worries of Ma and Pa resurfaced. Feelings of helplessness and guilt washed over me because I wasn't able to protect them from pain. Surely they couldn't have withstood the brutalities I'd endured. I wondered if they were even alive, and if so, where they were. I hoped my sister Willie and brother-in-law Koo had found a safe place to hide.

Once in a while I heard voices, though even by listening intently I couldn't make out what they said. At least I knew that I wasn't completely alone in my tomb. When it became silent again, hunger dominated my thoughts. Visions of grain blowing in the wind reminded me of those vast fields of wheat Pa and I had seen from the train on the trip we'd taken to the Ukraine to buy grain for his bread factory. We'd gone in 1937 when I was fourteen years old. What an impression those endless grain fields made on me and what I would give right now to have some bread from that grain.

My memories drifted on to bicycle trips I'd taken throughout Europe—freedom, friends, food, laughter, adventure. This should be the life of a nineteen year old. When I'd gotten into my teen years my parents had encouraged me to travel on my own. At first my schoolmates and I had taken short trips to Belgium and France. Gradually our trips had gotten longer: to Norway, Sweden, Germany, Austria, Switzerland, and Italy. We'd fastened sleeping bags, a pup tent, food, some pans and a small stove to our bike racks and hit the road. We'd pedal for a while, stop in a village, and visit historic sites, especially battle grounds. Sometimes we'd buy bread and meat from shops and put together sandwiches. It was easy to make friends, and some of these new friends would invite us into their homes for a meal and occasionally to spend the night. When motorists offered us rides, we'd hitch our bikes on to the back of trucks and make even faster tracks down the road. My mouth watered at the thought of sampling the food specialties of various countries—German bratwurst, French breads and pastries, and the ice cream, yogurt and cheese varieties of each country. These trips had also given me a chance to practice the languages I'd learned in school. If only I could feel the wind in my hair and the sun on my back as I had then.

When I'd returned from my most recent trip to Germany, I'd talked with my father. "Something is wrong. I felt an ugliness, an evilness in the air."

"Your mother and I have listened to Hitler rant and rave on the radio. But I think the German people are too smart to fall for his radical ideas," Pa reassured me. "Son, I think we learned our lesson from World War I. In any case, I served in the Dutch Army and we never fired a shot. Like Switzerland, no one wants our little country."

I wondered if my father ever thought of those words now. He was good at sizing up situations, but this time he'd missed the mark.

In my cell, hour after hour felt like year after year. After what I'd guessed to be two days, I'd gotten used to my own stench, but my bones felt as if they had broken into a hundred pieces. It drove me crazy to know I couldn't stand, sit or even stretch out. I kicked the wall and beat my fists bloody against the cement. Exhausted, I finally fell into a stupor.

After what seemed like a lifetime, guards pulled me from the cell. I didn't know what time or day it was. In the darkness guards dragged my numb body to another building and gave me some brown water. It tasted like champagne.

"You've had three days in *einselhaft*, 'solitary confinement,'" a guard informed me. "You're lucky. Nearly ninety percent of men sentenced to 'The Hole' die."

For several days I walked around in a daze. My fellow prisoners were surprised to see me again.

Not long after, a guard walked into our barracks. "We need a barber," he shouted.

He pulled me from the block and took me to the receiving building and put me to work. I recalled the procedure from my own experience. It didn't take much skill.

My first client was a small Jewish man who had little hair to begin with. We were not allowed to talk, but soulful eye and facial expressions said volumes. We shared a common misery that could only be understood by someone who had experienced similar agony.

I don't know how many haircuts I gave that day, but my hands were extremely sore that night, as they were in the days to follow. My reputation as a barber must have spread, because one night a German soldier ran into our block and yelled, "Where's the barber?"

I didn't know what to expect. I came forward and followed the soldier to the barbershop.

The soldier took off his cap, sat in a chair and said, *Nur ein wenig,* "Give me a trim. I have a date with a girl in Weimar." Weimar was a town about five miles south of Buchenwald.

Tempted as I was to give him a prison haircut, I resisted and tried to trim the edges. The smell of alcohol on his breath made me nervous.

He kept repeating, *"Nur ein wenig,"* and took the revolver out of his holster.

"I don't have a comb," I said in German.

He put his gun back in his holster and searched his pockets for a comb.

At that instant I thought, *Kill him. Take his uniform and escape. He's about my size and I know where he's going.*

He handed me the comb.

My hesitation had robbed me of a chance to flee. As I continued to cut, I cursed myself and thought, *am I too cowardly to try an escape?* I knew I'd let a rare opportunity pass.

When I'd finished, he took me back to my block. I didn't think his girlfriend would be impressed with his haircut. It looked as if a rat had chewed on his hair.

When I entered my block, several prisoners asked where I'd been. "We thought you'd been taken to the infirmary to be used as a guinea pig." I told them about the haircut, but not about the thoughts I'd had of escape.

As the days went by I became even more obsessed with breaking out. Every day I spent hours trying to figure out a plan. It was impossible to climb over the fence, going anywhere near it was suicide. A trigger-happy guard would be only too happy to kill any prisoner who got near the barbed wire. In December the weather became unbearably cold and more prisoners escaped life by running toward the fence. I seriously considered it, but held off thinking that maybe I'd get another chance at freedom.

One morning I woke up feeling so bad I thought I would die. I could hardly stand. I knew the rule of the camp: "We have no sick people here." I forced myself to stand through the frigid interminable roll call and through my job as a barber. At dinner I had to choke down the black bread. That night when I closed my eyes, I hoped they'd never open.

Morning came. I felt like I couldn't survive another day. During roll call, a Frenchman next to me whispered, "You have dysentery. The best way to cure that is to chew on burned wood. There is a piece outside the barracks. Trust me, but don't tell anybody I'm a doctor. If the SS find out they'll make me work on experiments with serums and drugs."

I found the piece of burned wood and chewed on it like it was a candy bar. After cutting hair that day I was glad to lie down, but by the next morning I felt better.

A Jewish prisoner came to me and said, "You were really sick yesterday. I expected you to be dead this morning."

So as not to betray the French doctor, I said, "Oh, yes. I'm okay now. I was my own doctor."

He misunderstood me and told others that I was a doctor. At first I didn't pay attention and went to the barbershop as usual and forgot about my remark.

Two days later, a German guard walked up to me and said, "We need doctors. Why didn't you tell us you were a doctor?"

"But I'm not a doctor," I insisted. I started to explain what had happened, when the guard belted me across the mouth with his gloved fist and knocked me to the ground. Spitting out my two front teeth, I shook off my dizziness and got up.

"Besides being a doctor, you're a liar," he screamed.

"Okay, I'm a doctor," I confessed, to keep the bastard from knocking me to the ground again.

Fourth betrayal, I thought at roll call. Probably at a cheap price too, a crust of bread or half a cigarette. Betrayal had gotten all too familiar. At dinner I studied each prisoner in our barracks, wondering which one was the traitor. I slept fitfully that night, every betrayer I'd ever known or heard of paraded through my dreams: The Dutch boy who'd joined the German army, quislings who'd sold out Jews, N.S.B.'ers who'd turned against their countrymen, German live-in maids who'd left just before the occupation taking with them photos and diaries filled with anti-Nazi statements made by their employers, the person who'd told of the underground's hiding place in the cemetery, the traitor at school, Rieta, and now a fellow prisoner. Life had become almost too much to bear.

Now I'd change careers and go from being an untrained barber to an untrained doctor. How insane could life get? A doctor at age nineteen. But I had not seen myself in a mirror for a long time and maybe by now I looked much older. Especially with two front teeth missing. Would I ever look like a young man again?

As I saw the black night turn to gray dawn through the dirty windows of our barracks, I thought, *Oh, God. What are the Nazis going to make me do now?*

CHAPTER VIII

The Butchershop

FTER MORNING ROLL CALL a guard took me to the hospital block, the infamous Block 46. It should have been named the "Butchershop." Here I met the also infamous Dr. Ding, director of the hospital, of whom I'd already heard many bad rumors. He was about as much like the doctor who'd set my broken arm when I was a kid as that brown water they served us was like coffee.

On my tour of the wards I saw prisoners crying and groaning, the pitiful sounds coming from their cadaverous bodies the only sign that they were alive. It didn't take a doctor to know that they wouldn't last long. We in the barracks thought our bodies were skin and bones, but these prisoners looked like cheesecloth-draped skeletons. It was incomprehensible.

Later that day I found out that these Jewish prisoners from Block 58 had been used as guinea pigs to try out new serums. Dr. Ding ordered me to cut open these test patients and remove their vital organs. When I made an incision in the first body, I felt unbearable pain, horror, repulsion and indescribable anguish. I dropped the knife and leaned against the table, my head spinning, bile churning in my stomach. I couldn't go on.

Dr. Ding stalked over. He cursed, kicked me in the rear end, and ordered me to cut out the heart before it spoiled. The Jew's eyes were sunk back into his head. He was dead, but his body still felt warm. With trembling hands I separated the ribs and cut out the heart. Either Dr. Ding or his staff didn't notice or didn't care that my cuts were not precise like a surgeon's. A staff member took the heart and boxed it in dry ice. I heard that the hearts and lungs were sent to Berlin for further examination to determine the effects of the serums.

I don't know how I ever made it through that first day. Most patients didn't move with the first thrust of the knife, but one quivered as I cut him open. He was alive! Again I stopped unable to go on. Tears came to my eyes and I gripped the table to keep from charging out of the room. Dr. Ding rushed to my side, screaming for me to continue. As the day wore on I tried to console myself. *They would die anyway. Now at least they were out of their misery.*

Every day and every night I became more determined to find a way to escape this stinking hole of a camp. Each imagined attempt seemed to be impossible. As Christmas approached, I didn't know how much longer I could do the horrendous things I was forced to do in the name of being a doctor. One day at the hospital I had to surgically remove tattoos. I couldn't figured out what they were used for. Later I heard that the wife of SS Col. Karl Koch, commander of Buchenwald, saved these patches of tattooed skin. Ilsa Koch, known as the "Bitch of Buchenwald," stretched these skins over a frame to shape them into lamp shades. American soldiers discovered a collection of her lamp shades after the liberation of Buchenwald in April of 1945.

Another day I strapped leech-filled boxes to the legs of prisoners to test if leeches took poison out of the blood. Around the same time I and other doctors were forced to cut the fingertips off of several Jews. The tips were reattached to see if they would regrow. I never heard the results of either experiment.

Yet another day I operated on Jewish prisoners who had died in high G-loading experiments. In a centrifuge they were brought to a force of nine or ten Gs to see how many Gs a body could tolerate. When the dead bodies were hauled out, I removed the heart and lungs, which were again boxed and sent to Berlin for examination.

Before long I could tell by the expressions on the prisoners faces how many Gs they had been taken to. After the war I and the rest of the world found out that these experiments were early attempts to prepare man for space flight. The Germans had already invented rockets. The next step would be to put men aboard.

These days I was nothing more than a butcher. As time passed I became desensitized to my tasks. Yet I knew deep down inside what I was doing was wrong.

With Christmas a few days away, I heard more prisoners praying out loud during the night. One called out, "Christ is coming on His birthday and we'll all be set free." With all that we'd experienced, I found their faith difficult to understand. Not having a strong religious background, I didn't know many prayers. However, hearing so many prisoners talking to the Lord with joy in their voices aroused my curiosity. We held hands, forming a chain between sleeping platforms. In my awkward way I tried to pray.

A believer told me, "If we are united in the Lord, He will destroy the devil," the devil being the Nazis. I got some comfort from these group prayers, but I'm not sure how much I believed that the Lord would save us. I'd come to the conclusion that each of us was on his own.

Christmas Eve day I stood in roll call, just having dragged two dead prisoners out, one on each side of me. After roll call ended and the dead bodies had been thrown forward, I noticed a German guard toss away his cigarette butt. I pretended to fall so I could save the butt to trade for a piece of bread. The guard saw me, stepped on my hand and whacked me on the head with a club.

I woke up in "The Hole."

"Oh, my God. Not again! I cried. "I'll never survive three days in this coffin." My heart pounded so hard I thought I would choke on my heartbeat. I panted uncontrollably. After a long time my breathing and heartbeat returned to normal.

My hand hurt, but because the cigarette butt had fallen on mud the guard hadn't broken my hand when he'd stepped on it. My upper lip was swollen like a balloon and my gums, where my two front teeth had been knocked out earlier, were infected. I sucked out the foul-tasting pus to get some liquid.

I didn't know how long I'd been unconscious, but from the moment I regained consciousness every minute seemed like a century. Thinking back on my first hellish imprisonment in "The Hole," I became convinced that my only way out was as a corpse.

Then I heard singing, as if I'd died and gone to heaven. Straining, I could just make out snatches of, "Tannenbaum, oh Tannenbaum, wie grun . . ." It lasted for only a few minutes. At first I couldn't believe it. Did Nazis believe in Christmas? How could they when they acted so unchristian. Or were they just using the occasion as an excuse to get drunk? Even if they were, I enjoyed the music while it lasted. As the day wore on, I thought of Christmases my family had celebrated in the past.

I remembered one in particular. I was a young boy and we had decorated the tree with ornaments and candles. Each candle sat on a round metal holder which we'd clipped to the branches. I drew and cut out a church and placed it over a lit candle because I wanted the light to shine through. The church caught on fire. Pa sprang up, ran for a pail of water and threw it on the tree. Ma complained that our Persian rug would never be the same. Later we'd laughed, but at the time it had been quite a serious matter. Another time I'd knocked the tree over chasing Jony, our fox terrier, around the apartment. That act didn't win me any popularity contests, and Willie never let me forget either incident.

My intense thirst brought me back to reality. As on my first time in solitary confinement, I urinated on the wall and licked the liquid off as well as cement particles. It must have been early the next morning when guards pulled me out.

"We need a doctor," one of them said.

After letting me get some water, they took me to the Butchershop where a guard who'd smashed his thumb in a truck door waited. I found a burner and a needle and heated it until it was red hot. Tempted though I was to insert that needle where it would do even more damage, I used it to poke the black nail and release the trapped blood. I'd learned this trick from all the times Pa had drained the blood from my many blackened thumb nails. At least being a doctor had gotten me out of "The Hole" early.

The week passed and 1943 began, but I'd come no closer to finding a way to escape. I felt weaker all the time and thought my weight had dropped below one hundred pounds. These days there was little conversation in our barracks. God had not come to free us on His Son's birthday. Still that didn't discourage some religious prisoners from asking us to join them in prayer, although praying was absolutely forbidden by the Nazis. I guess to these prisoners it didn't matter anymore. Most were as close to death as they could get and still be alive.

One night a prisoner led us in prayer saying, "Our Father, Who art in heaven . . ." A chorus of voices joined him. When he came to "Give us this day our daily bread" many prisoners choked on the words. The undertone clearly meant, God, look at our starving, feverish bodies. Can you help us? The prayer continued, "And forgive us our trespasses as we forgive our 'torturers of thousands' everyday. And lead us not into temptation—today the despair of millions—but deliver us from evil, from all the suffering we've endured for months. Amen." After the voices faded away I felt calmer, though I still had doubts that a loving God existed.

A few mornings later, a Kapo grabbed a Belgian doctor and me by the arms saying, "We need doctors in Block 46."

The Belgian doctor asked me in Flemish, "I wonder what our Doctor Ding is up to now?"

"Something terrible you can be sure."

"Speak only German," the Kapo ordered.

Block 46 was well known to be the testing laboratory for illnesses like diphtheria, typhus and dysentery. When we arrived, a line of fourteen or fifteen Jews awaited us. A small box lay on the table. The Belgian doctor and I were ordered to inject the serum. He looked at me, his eyes delivering an unmistakable message—fake it. By this time I'd gotten very adept at reading eye and facial expressions.

We filled our needles from the little bottles. Acting as if we were injecting the full dose, we emptied most of the serum into their clothing, then pressed just hard enough to leave a needle impression. The Jews acted their parts, pulling their faces in pain. That day I learned a valuable lesson—act strong and don't be scared. By looking into the eyes of those Jews, I gained a lot of confidence. They gave me the courage to hang on to life. Saving lives rather than taking them left me feeling triumphant. Jews in the experiment later told us that the serum was typhus and that they'd been given extra rations for taking part in the experiment. I worried that because the Jews never got typhus the Germans might get suspicious, but nothing ever came of it.

One of Hitler's hatchet men, Heinrich Himmler, head of the SS and Gestapo, often came to Buchenwald to request experiments. When he did, camp officers shook in their boots in fear that if they didn't please him he'd send them to fight on the Russian front. The officers knew that torturing prisoners was much easier duty than fighting in a war.

That winter Himmler arrived in camp to initiate experiments on how to save the limbs of frostbitten soldiers. I stood about twenty feet from him. Like Dr. Ding he was a short man who wore glasses. Both seemed to act big and tough to make up for their small stature. As a doctor I became involved in Himmler's experiments. I didn't find out until later that by early 1943 the war on the eastern front was going badly for the Germans. Frigid winter weather had caused serious frostbite among the troops, and Himmler had been assigned to solve the frostbite problem. I also learned later that Russian soldiers knew to put grease on their faces to keep out the cold and prevent frostbite.

Buchenwald scientists designed an experiment. In the first round of the experiment, the infirmary staff threw prisoners into a pool of ice and left them until they were unconscious. Upon pulling out the bodies, blankets were thrown over the prisoners to warm them. All the bodies turned black and the prisoners died. In the next round of the experiment, more prisoners were thrown into the ice pool. This time, upon being pulled out, they were immersed in tepid water. Again all the prisoners died.

On the third round, after pulling the unconscious prisoners out of the pool, the staff immersed them in very warm water. This time the prisoners survived. Besides acting as a doctor in this experiment, I also acted as a guinea pig. An SS guard thought he was being funny and with a big grin shoved me into the pool. When I landed in the pool, I hoped I'd survive because the frostbite problem had already been solved. All of the times I'd swum in the North Sea into late fall must have made my body more tolerant of cold water.

Life was cheap: death by starvation, beatings, shootings, suicide or experiments occurred daily. Now not a day went by that a prisoner did not run for the fence to end his life. Such a large number of prisoners died that I'd smell sickening smoke trailing from the chimney of the crematorium day and night. And I'd yet to see the worst.

One day I saw a prison worker, one of the crew who did clean-up in Block 46, slip the liver of a dead Jew into his pocket. I had a sudden hideous image of him hiding in a corner of his barracks eating that liver. My stomach nearly turned inside-out in revulsion. And even worse, I had to believe that this was not the first time cannibalism had taken place. With rampant hunger, liver theft might occur often. I'd just never witnessed it before. For days I walked around in numb silence. I wondered why no one told on the thief to get more rations or cigarettes. Maybe the thief shared the liver? After that first time I often saw workers sneak out livers.

For me to survive would be a miracle. I tried to find people I knew, but in vain. Sammy's father disappeared in the crowd of skeletal faces. Our bodies had deteriorated so badly that even if I'd seen someone I knew, it would be impossible to recognize him or for him to recognize me.

There was no way that any of us could know how the war was going. Planes frequently flew over, but it was difficult to distinguish the Germans from the British or Americans. Occasionally we'd hear bombs drop, but we never heard any follow-up information. The only time we knew of problems was when a German leader like Himmler came into camp.

I still hoped to escape and had long ago figured out which direction was which. The weather became warmer, but not quite warm enough. I couldn't hold out much longer. My body felt weak though I could still move around.

I nearly gave up my struggle to survive on the day I walked out the back door of Block 46 and saw several Jews hanging from twelve foot tall poles. Their hands were tied with wire behind their backs and around the pole. Their full body weight hung from their hands. They dangled only two feet off the ground, but were totally helpless. Most drooped forward, unconscious. Others grimaced so painfully it would be only a short time before they blacked out. Images of Jesus hanging from the cross flashed to mind. Could the Nazis be punishing the Jews for crucifying Jesus? But some professed not to believe in God or Jesus Christ. More likely they had chosen this torture because it was especially cruel.

My worst nightmare came true when the Nazis hung me from one of those twelve foot poles. All I'd done was ask a Jew if he knew a Mr. Cohen, Sammy's father. It had never occurred to me that this was a crime worthy of the severest punishment. Yet within minutes guards grabbed me, shoved me up against a pole, yanked my arms behind me and around the pole. I didn't have the strength to fight them off. One guard twisted wire tightly around my wrists while the other held me still. Then both guards slid me up the pole several feet and let me drop. Excruciating pain shot through my hands, wrists, and arms. Within minutes I'd passed out.

I had no idea how long I'd hung there unconscious. I only regained consciousness when a guard cut me down. My right wrist had been cut to the bone. I felt sure that once I'd healed I would carry the scar from this torture for the rest of my life, however long that might be. I'd reached the point, mentally and physically, where I could not endure any more tortures. *Hell would seem like heaven to me after what I'd seen and experienced.* I had to do something. Now.

Soon after, on a night in mid-March, I lay awake the entire night trying to gather courage to make my move. The day before, I'd noticed that the crematorium was closed down and found out that coal supplies had run out. This fact, along with a flashback of an earlier prisoner on my block who'd pretended to be dead, galvanized my plan. When I'd picked up this prisoner in the morning he felt different, like he was still alive. I treated him as I would have treated any other dead body I'd dragged to roll call. At the end of roll call I told the guard, "Er ist tot," and threw his body forward. I prayed my fellow prisoners would do the same favor for me.

I'd been cautioned several times that less than ten people had ever escaped from Buchenwald since 1937. It didn't matter anymore.

That March night I made up my mind to attempt an escape or to die trying.

CHAPTER IX

Escape

THAT NIGHT LASTED an eternity. At dawn I lay motionless on my platform while other prisoners crawled out at the guard's call. Men dying during the night was common, so I wasn't given a second glance. As a prisoner dragged me to roll call, I concentrated on keeping my body as limp as possible. After the interminable roll call, the prisoner dropped me forward and shouted, "Er ist tot." I knew that once on the ground I couldn't move, so during the fall I turned my head to the side so I could breathe. I wondered if my barracks mate suspected I had faked death.

A few minutes later a truck with a front-end loader scooped me up along with the other bodies. In the jostling, I lifted one eyelid to see where we were going. After passing through a gate, the driver positioned us over a pile of bodies in the crematorium yard and dumped us. As I fell I managed to get into position to endure a long wait. I felt hopeful just to have gotten this far.

As the guards circled the mound of bodies, I listened to check out how many soldiers were on duty. It wasn't long before a guard shot into the pile of prisoners. My body twitched involuntarily. Ten minutes later another shot hit a body a short distance away, shaking me up again. I felt lucky the guards hadn't noticed me. I let myself fall into a stupor as I'd done in "The Hole." During the morning several more shots were fired, but none near me. By then I'd gotten better at not reacting.

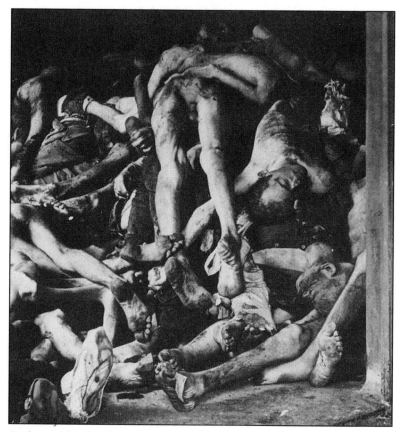

Buchenwald body pile, waiting near crematorium.

As the morning wore on, I'd figured out by the guards' footsteps that there were six of them. Several left for lunch. Some did not return. By now I'd played dead for six hours and my body felt completely paralyzed. To moisten my dry mouth, I pressed my upper lip against my infected gums and forced out the pus and swallowed it. This only helped for a short time.

Earlier that morning the warm bodies laying against me helped to keep me warm. Gradually they cooled. By mid-day I figured only two guards remained. Time crept so slowly it almost stopped. Several arms and legs lay like pick-up sticks across me, so between the passing of the guards I tried to stretch out my limbs. My mind was still going strong, but I feared my body had stiffened so badly that I wouldn't be able to move when I needed to. I'd been lying still since about 5:00 A.M. and now it must be nearly 6:00 P.M. My whole life had passed before me many times.

In my mind I heard the prisoners in my barracks praying at night. *What good did it do? Here they were lying dead next to me. There couldn't be a God who would allow this to happen. Or he must love our damned enemies more that the innocent men around me.* I was on my own and had to make my move soon or die on this rotting heap of carcasses.

Slowly I opened my eyes, trying to locate the guards. Now I heard only one guard circling. I counted to find out how long it took for him to make his rounds.

The day was dreary, but there had been no rain. As the temperature grew cooler, the time it took the guard to circle grew longer. Still I hadn't figured out how I would make my break. I heard voices. The guard changed, and now I had to figure out how long it took the new guard to walk his circuit.

The sun set. I thought it better to go for it in the dark. I'd gotten so thirsty I couldn't lie still any longer. I no longer cared what happened.

While the guard circled around the back side of the pile I shifted into a position to spring. After he passed, I jumped up, bashed him on the shoulder and knocked him to the ground popping off his helmet. I grabbed the helmet and beat him over the head with it until I was sure he was dead. Panting from exertion, I rolled him over, tugged off his boots, coat and pants and put them on. Suddenly—silence. For the first time in years I was unafraid.

The uniform fit like a tent, but his suspenders helped keep the pants off my heels. After I'd undressed the soldier, I dragged him to the pile and pulled other bodies on top of him. I wondered what the prisoners who loaded dead bodies into the ovens at the crematorium would think when they found this healthy body among the dead prisoners? I'd bet at least one prisoner would figure out that the body was a German soldier and realize a prisoner had killed him. I could see the crematorium worker smile and comment that at least one lucky SOB had made it out alive.

I felt weight in the coat pocket. I reached in and pulled out a flask, one of the best gifts I'd ever received in my life. I must have grinned like a boy who had gotten away with skipping school by pretending to be sick. I took a little sip and swished the burning liquor around in my mouth and slowly let it slide down my throat. My gums no longer hurt. After pocketing the soldier's flask, I pulled out his garrison cap and put it on. I ditched the unneeded helmet under some bodies. I hoped I looked like an off-duty soldier.

There I stood in a German uniform, looking quite grotesque, at least at close range. Hefting the guard's rifle over my shoulder I headed toward the guardhouse. I'd seen German soldiers take trucks and leave the camp for nearby towns. That was probably how the soldier who's hair I'd trimmed had planned to get to Weimar. Maybe I could sneak onto the back of a truck and get through the gate. As I walked around for a few minutes, a truck unexpectedly pulled out from behind a building and stopped next to me.

My heart beat wildly. If I hadn't had on three layers of clothes, I'm sure the driver and his soldier passenger would have seen my heart fluttering under my shirt.

The driver opened the door a crack, and said loudly over the roar of the engine, "Nach Weimar?"

"Ja," I yelled back.

I walked to the back of the truck and crawled onto the empty bed. Thank God for the black paper covering the truck's headlights. I was convinced that if the driver and his friend had seen me in full light, they'd have known I was an escapee. I sat down, leaned my back against the cab and heaved a huge sigh. The vehicle started forward.

Two more stops until freedom. Did I dare to hope? At the first guardhouse the soldier came out with a flashlight and checked over the truck. As the light passed over me, I gave him a friendly wave. He motioned the driver on. The guard at the final guardhouse waved us through.

"Thank God, thank God, thank God. I've escaped Buchenwald!"

I realized what I'd just said and knew God had helped me. He wasn't on vacation after all. A ninety pound man by himself could never have overpowered and killed a German soldier twice his weight. *Calm down,* I cautioned myself, *you're not safe yet.* On the twenty minute ride to Weimar I thought about what I would do when I got there.

When the driver slowed on the outskirts of Weimar, I jumped off the truck, waved to the soldiers and kept on moving out of town. I'd be safer in the country. Where my energy came from I don't know, because I hadn't had any food or water for more than twenty-four hours. But I continued to run south at a steady pace for four miles until I saw a farmhouse. By this time my confidence must have been *spitze,* at an all-time high.

I knocked, and a thin middle-aged woman immediately opened the door.

"Good evening. I'm lost and I need a drink."

"Come in," she said, and led me to the kitchen. In the brighter light I could see that jaw surgery had altered one side of her still pretty face.

Her husband nodded at me, but didn't rise from the table where he sat smoking a pipe. A black Dutch cap sat on his head. His bushy eyebrows protruded over his glasses as he studied me with curious blue eyes.

I thanked her for the water. "I'm also hungry. Would you have any extra food?"

"I baked bread this morning." She set a loaf on the table.

The couple didn't seem intimidated by my rifle, but I was prepared to use it if I had to. Probably seeing German soldiers was a normal thing for them.

I sat down and in minutes had devoured the fresh delicious bread.

The kind woman smiled. "We have some leftovers from dinner." She tucked a strand of blond hair into a bun at the back of her head. "Would you like them? My husband and I are getting older and don't eat as much anymore."

I don't remember what I ate, but I polished off everything the woman offered. When I had finished, the farmer tapped out his pipe and asked, "So you're lost?" and started to give me all kinds of directions.

His wife interrupted. "Do you have to leave tonight? Could you wait until morning? You could use our son's bedroom. He's away in the army."

"Thank you. I'd like to stay." After the treatment I'd received I trusted the couple. Either that or I felt so dead on my feet that I didn't care anymore.

"I hate to impose on you again," I said, "but I could use a bath."

The farmer's wife heated water and filled the tub which was located in a small room off the kitchen next to the stairs. In the luxury of the warm water I relaxed so completely that I almost fell asleep. The quiet voices of the couple talking in the kitchen sounded like a lullaby. I thoroughly enjoyed my first real bath and bed in almost seven months. It took a while to get to sleep. My stomach gurgled and churned on the huge amount of food I'd eaten. Finally I fell asleep and didn't wake up until mid-morning the following day.

I sat up, looked around and noticed a closet. I got up, checked inside and found their son's clothing, and in a drawer some underwear. I helped myself to clean underwear, a shirt, trousers, and a jacket, all pretty close to my size. Over the top I put on the German soldier's uniform. As I buttoned the uniform, I studied several photos on the wall. The same young man was pictured in each: with his family, with classmates, alone in a German Army uniform. Their son, I thought, and went down to breakfast.

What luck that I had ended up on a farm. The farmer's wife fixed ham and eggs for me. While I ate, her husband rolled up his flannel shirtsleeves and drew a map on the table with his finger to the nearest village and beyond. "Could you use an old bicycle?" he asked. "It would be much faster."

I thanked them profusely. After this offer, I felt sure that this couple knew more than they had let on. In their quiet way they protested against the policies of their government. For that reason I left no trace that I had been there. I even stuffed my stinking prison rags inside my uniform to dispose of later. It was heartwarming to know that not all Germans believed and acted like the Nazis.

Before I left, the farmer gripped my hand in a strong handshake. I kissed his wife good-bye. When I swung onto the bicycle, the couple stood in the doorway to see me off. The woman made the sign of the cross. This surprised me because I hadn't seen a single religious symbol in the house.

Little did I know that before the war had ended I would return their favor when I met their son.

CHAPTER X

Freedom

As I pedaled briskly down the road I broke into a sweat. In the first culvert I stuffed my prison clothes; in the next one I hid the German soldier's uniform and rifle. Shedding this extra baggage made me feel almost naked. To my surprise I found a wallet in my new trousers. Further down the road I buried the wallet and folded the thirty marks into my pocket. "Thank you," I said gratefully to my benefactor.

A damp earth smell of early spring filled my nostrils as I rode through the countryside. Occasionally I passed a tree or saw farm buildings in the distance, but met up with no other people.

Feeling like a new man, I arrived at the village of Vieselbach. That morning I'd run my hand through my prison head stubble and decided I'd better cover it, so bought a cap. After I'd looked around town I began to feel conspicuous, because the only men there were those too old to serve in the military. I traded my "new man" status for that of a bent, limping ex-soldier recovering from a war wound. Practicing my new gait, I hobbled into a bakery.

"Do you have anything I can get without coupons?" I asked the motherly woman behind the counter.

She showed me some crackers.

The aroma of fresh baked bread nearly had me drooling on the counter, and after my prison diet I didn't want to settle for crackers.

"Could I give you extra money for a loaf of bread? Or do you have bread crumbs that you could sell without coupons?"

She looked me up and down with alert blue eyes and must have felt sorry for me because she handed me a loaf of bread without charging me a penny.

"Thank you very much. Is there any work I could do to help out?"

"No, thank you," she said. "And good luck."

Outside the shop I broke off a piece of bread, ate it and washed it down with a swallow from the Buchenwald guard's flask. The liquor deadened my still infected gums. Then I completed my transformation to a civilian with a stop at the shoe store. On my way out of town I ditched the too-big army boots in a trash can.

Exhilarated, I rode toward Erfurt, full and unafraid. Once out of town I dropped my disguise and pedaled at top speed. The sun's warmth on my back and shoulders, penetrating through partly cloudy skies, felt like a massage. This feeling of comfort brought back memories of bike rides Ma, Pa, Willie and I had taken along the coast of Holland. Like a spring ritual, we'd bicycled for hours between tulip fields. After a picnic lunch, Willie and I would tie up strings of red, pink and yellow tulips and weave them around the handlebars and frames of our bikes. On the ride home we'd meet up with other children who'd decorated their bikes. The group of us would wave regally to pedestrians as if we were in a parade.

The memory of my family stirred up mixed feelings in me—the happiness of shared experiences and the fear that we'd never again be a whole family. As the months had passed in Buchenwald, I'd thought less and less about Ma, Pa and Willie. It had become too painful. I didn't want to believe they'd experienced the same horrors that I had, because I knew they couldn't have lived through them. And I couldn't face the thought that they were dead.

To survive I had to immediately get the hell out of Germany by heading west by southwest as the farmer had suggested. He'd said it would take a day to reach Erfurt, the nearest town with a railroad. The old bike and I were doing fine, but riding a bike would not be fast enough.

By now the sun dipped low on the western horizon and my ears worked overtime to pick up the sound of a train. Only once all day had I seen a military vehicle, and I'd heard it early enough to duck into a ditch and hide myself and the bicycle. That encounter was a convincing reminder that I was still in enemy territory and had better stay watchful. As the miles had rolled by, I was surprised at the amount of energy I had gained since escaping from Buchenwald.

Darkness settled in and because of the blackout it was difficult to spot a town from a distance. Suddenly I heard voices and knew I'd reached Erfurt. The sound of the coupling and uncoupling of boxcars guided me to the railroad station. In the dark it took me a long time to figure out which train would head west. Once I'd chosen a train, I walked past a dozen closed boxcars until I found one with a missing door. I couldn't force myself to get into an empty closed car. They triggered images of dead prisoners being hauled out from them like I'd seen after my train ride from Vught to Weimar. In fact they smelled the same as the one I traveled in to Buchenwald. I didn't think I'd ever climb into a closed boxcar again. I wondered if these empty boxcars were headed west to be filled with more unsuspecting prisoners destined for Buchenwald.

I breathed deeply, trying to calm myself. I lifted my bike into the open car and crawled in after it. I settled into a corner, ate some bread, sipped some liquor and fell asleep. It must have been a deep sleep, because when I woke up the train was moving and daylight slanted into the open door.

I studied the shadows cast by fence posts and buildings to confirm that the train was headed west. It was. At each stop I'd peek out to see if soldiers were coming to check the cars. Luck was with me. I saw no one. With each mile from Buchenwald I grew happier. After one long stop I settle in for a nap until dawn. This time I woke up in Koblenz, a large German city, noisy with clanging trains and honking cars.

Here I switched to a train that sped me southwest through the night until we reached a mid-sized city, Trier. Trier was located on a river about twenty-five miles from the French border. Suddenly the train screeched to a halt throwing me forward onto my face. Overhead in the darkness I heard the whine of diving planes and the rattle of artillery fire. Thinking that the allies were bombing the station, I picked myself up and jumped to the ground.

A German soldier trotting by grabbed my arm and led me away from the train station. *I'm done for,* I thought. My heart beat at double time. *I should kill him now.* Lucky for me I didn't act upon my thoughts.

Insistently the soldier pulled me toward some buildings and said, "Go down those stairs." By then bombs were falling all around us.

I stumbled down the stairs, lit only by a red exit light, and realized this was a bomb shelter. The German soldier had saved my life. In the faint light I caught a glimpse of his face, not the menacing face of a Nazi guard, but a more gentle and trustworthy one.

Overhead planes continued to attack the city. By now my eyes had adjusted to the dim light of the basement room. I saw three other soldiers in the shelter. We nodded greetings, but none of us introduced ourselves.

My escort—I mentally called him Sarge—was excited. His nervous chatter almost drowned out the noise of the air attack.

"I can't wait until the war is over," said Sarge. "I'm a baker in Munich, and if you ever come to my town after the war, look me up. I'll bake you a cake." He talked about his family and plans for the future.

For me Sarge put an every day face on soldiers in the war. He was a husband and father, doing a job he enjoyed to support his family. I hoped he survived the war to get back to his family and bakery shop in Munich.

Finally the air attack ended and Sarge and the other soldiers fell asleep. Feeling ungrateful, yet desperately hungry, I slipped Sarge's knapsack out from under the bench where he'd stowed it, tiptoed upstairs and outside. Quickly I checked the contents of the pack and was overjoyed to find three bottles of French cognac, bread, bratwurst and two packages of cigarettes. I thanked Sarge for coming to my rescue once again.

Daylight filtered through the cloud cover. I couldn't walk around Trier long without creating suspicion, so returned to the train and discovered my bike was gone. The air attack had done little damage to the railroad station. To avoid meeting up with Sarge, I hopped the first train that moved. I had no time to choose the direction, and sure enough the train headed north toward Belgium and The Netherlands. My heart ached to get home, but I knew I wouldn't be safe there. In the town of Aachen, Belgium, I reluctantly boarded a southbound train. I settled in for a long ride. picnicking on the bratwurst, bread and cognac. Even though I was still in occupied territory I could relax a little knowing that trains weren't checked at every town. After the train passed through Liege and Bastogne, Belgium, and into France, I arbitrarily got off in the town of Neufchateau.

I wanted to stretch my legs on a walk through this beautiful French town of nine castles, but eating the bread and bratwurst had caused my gums to swell horribly. Even the cognac didn't deaden the pain anymore. I walked down the main street, avoiding anyone in uniform. Above a doorway I saw a sign; Dr. Marvell, Dentist. I paused a moment, wondering if it would be safe to go in. The pain gave me no choice. As I stepped into the office, I quickly checked to see if there were any German soldiers inside. There were none.

A nurse sat at her desk drinking coffee. "Do you have an . . ." she started to ask. One look at my face and she jumped up and said, "The doctor will be out in a minute."

After notifying the dentist, she poured me a cup of coffee. Before I'd had time to take a sip, the dentist appeared and said, "Come in." He motioned me into the adjoining room and into the dental chair. This man, only slightly shorter than I, checked me over with concern. While he examined my mouth I looked into his brown eyes and at his clean-shaven face to see if I could trust him.

"What happened?" he asked. "Been running from the Germans? Where are you from and where are you going?"

I felt safe confiding in him, and confident that at Buchenwald I'd learned a lot about reading peoples' eyes and expressions accurately.

"I'm a Dutchman and I've escaped from a concentration camp." He didn't ask for details.

"I have no money, but I could pay you later," I offered.

He ignored my remark and got busy. "I'll have to lance your gums." He worked for an hour. When he had finished he asked, "What is your name?"

"Jacques," I answered.

"Jacque, are you FFI or Marquis?"

From my days in the Dutch underground, I knew that these were two French resistance organizations. "Neither," I answered.

"I'm Marquis," Dr. Marvell confided.

By this time we'd established mutual trust, and I went on to tell him some of my story.

"Well, Jacque," said Dr. Marvell, "it will take several days for your gums to heal enough for me to finish the job. The roots are good, but the teeth are uneven, so I'll have to smooth them out. Then I'll drill holes and insert two false teeth using pegs."

"All right," I answered, wondering what I would do in the meantime.

"Do you have a place to stay?"

"No. I just arrived."

"Wait a minute," said Dr. Marvell, and left the room.

I had a sight twinge of nervousness. *Maybe I've told him too much.* His quick return and calm manner reassured me that I'd judged him correctly.

"My nurse made the arrangements," Dr. Marvell said. "Everything is set. You can stay at my house, but it will be safer if you go there after dark. For now you can wait here. My wife, Cherie, will be over soon with something to eat."

An hour later, Dr. Marvell's attractive wife brought soup and bread for us. This slender, dark haired woman hovered near. While I ate gingerly, she patted me on the back, saying, "God be with you." I felt God had already been, and that Dr. Marvell and his wife were quickly becoming true friends.

Later Dr. Marvell and I walked to his house. After I'd cleaned up, his wife served what seem like a gourmet dinner. The three of us talked for hours. I filled in the details of what had happened to me over the last seven months and told them a little about my family in The Netherlands.

Dr. Marvell shared some of his experiences. "I served in the French Army, but was discharged because I'm too old. When I returned home I started up my dental practice again and joined the French underground."

Feeling very safe and comfortable, I spent the next day resting, eating and being pampered by Mrs. Marvell. Just as talkative as her husband, she shared stories and photos of their daughter who was now married.

"I have a married sister." I went on to tell her about Willie's wedding and about her husband, Koo.

The next evening Dr. Marvell casually mentioned at dinner, "Tonight Francois is coming over. He's a member of the Marquis. But don't worry, Jacque," he added hastily. "He's a good friend."

When Francois entered the room, his commanding presence overpowered everything in it. He gave me a firm handshake, his penetrating brown eyes looking steadily into mine.

"Very glad to meet you, Jacque. Doc Vell told me about some of your experiences." Like the Marvells, he was easy to talk to and a good listener. He asked sympathetic questions about life in Buchenwald and my escape from there.

After we'd talked a while, I remembered the bottles of cognac in the knapsack I'd taken from Sarge. There was no need to save it for medicine as my gums were healing nicely. I went to get a bottle.

"What a treat this will be," said Dr. Marvell, examining the label.

"Where did you get it? asked Francois, as Dr. Marvell's wife brought glasses.

I told them the story of Sarge and we all enjoyed a hearty laugh.

"To Sarge," said Francois, raising his glass in a toast.

"Salud," we chorused.

"A gift from a German soldier. Now that's indeed an event to celebrate," said Dr. Marvell. He took another sip and swirled the liquor around in his mouth before swallowing it. Over the evening of talk we finished the bottle. The friendly conversation turned serious when Francois started telling me about the French underground.

"There's a real need for brave strong men in the Paris underground," said Francois. He leaned forward and brushed back his dark wavy hair. "They're involved with sabotage, evacuating downed Allied pilots, hiding Jews, and smuggling German dissenters out of the country." He looked me directly in the eyes. "Jacque, would you like to join?"

"Could I think about it?" I hadn't figured out what I'd do after my teeth were fixed. "I need time to look at my choices."

"Certainly," said Francois. "I'll contact you in a couple of days." He stood and shook hands. "Thanks for the cognac," he said, and left.

By the next day my gums were well enough healed for Doc Vell, as everyone called him, to cement in the two false teeth. With new front teeth and a weight gain I almost looked and felt nineteen again.

"You can't bite down on anything hard yet, so we're having soup again tonight." Regardless of your teeth that's what we'd have anyway," Doc said, and chuckled. "We can thank my wife and the vegetable garden she plants every spring."

After I'd enjoyed one more day of rest and good food, Francois returned. I had decided to join the French underground because I knew I couldn't go back to The Netherlands. Doc Vell had evidently told Francois this as he had already arranged a ride for me to Paris.

"How can I ever repay you?" I asked the Marvells the next morning as I prepared to leave.

"Jacque, you don't owe us anything," said Doc Vell. "It was a pleasure to help out a patriot who'll be fighting for the freedom of France. If you ever have a chance to return to Neufchateau, we'd love to see you."

"Thank you both for everything." I shook hands with Doc Vell and his wife. She kissed me on both cheeks in the French custom.

I climbed into the battered truck and off we started for Paris.

Escape from Buchenwald and route to Paris, France

CHAPTER XI

Paris Underground

I 'M PIERRE," said the truck driver, grinding the gears of the old truck. He was so short it was a stretch for him to push the clutch to the floorboard. "Glad to have you join us. You can ride up front for now, but when we reach Paris you'll have to climb in the back. You'll receive your counterfeit ID when we reach Paris."

After Pierre's long-winded speech I introduced myself. Still feeling some prison bred reluctance to share, I told him only a little about myself and changed the subject. "What are you hauling in the back of the truck?" I asked loudly over the rumble of the engine.

"I carry all kinds of supplies to the Paris underground." He continued as if answering a often asked question, "I can't fight because I have an enlarged heart and a missing kidney. So this is how I serve my country."

As we bounced toward Paris in the ancient truck, we shared our mutual hatred of the Nazis. Over the miles I grew as comfortable talking to Pierre as I had with Dr. and Mrs. Marvell and Francois.

"Tell me how it was in camp," encouraged Pierre.

Gradually I told him many of the sordid details of my days in Buchenwald.

"I've never heard anything so damned incredible in my life," said Pierre scratching the stubble on his chin. "While you were there did you hear any information about Germany's losses?"

"Very little," I answered. "We saw planes fly over, but of course the Germans didn't tell us anything."

"I'd like to know if any war machinery plants like the Krupp factory have been bombed?"

"I haven't heard. How are things going in France?"

"Not much has been bombed, but we're in bad shape because of food shortages," said Pierre. "Many Frenchmen are in the Resistance, but life seems hopeless at times. To get outside help looks to be impossible. The Germans have the coasts so well guarded."

I unwrapped the bread and cheese packed by Dr. Marvell's wife, and we lunched in the truck as we rattled down country roads. I felt hopeful for the future as I looked out the window—newborn calves nursed in pastures, vegetables popped up in freshly tilled gardens near farmhouses. The scene appeared peaceful, until German military trucks passed by filled with gun-toting soldiers.

Before we'd reached the outskirts of Paris, Pierre pulled onto the roadside and I climbed over the tailgate and into the canvas-covered truck bed. Only a crack in the back flap allowed me to see where we'd been. The back of the truck was in total darkness. Every time Pierre slowed for a stop sign or checkpoint, I crouched into position to hide behind some boxes. Hiding was unnecessary, as no soldier checked in the back of the truck.

The engine finally stopped and Pierre came around and opened the flap a crack. "Wait here until I talk to the leader."

After a long wait, Pierre returned. "It's safe," he said and gave me directions to a house. "Good luck."

"Thanks." I shook his hand. "And good luck to you."

I walked through a well established residential area of tall brick houses. In the distance I saw the Eiffel tower. Again was impressed, as I had been as a young boy, by it's strong slender profile. When I reached the house the door stood open. "Hello," I called.

A voice boomed from upstairs, "Come in. Come on up." A giant of a man met me at the top of the stairs and his hand engulfed mine in a handshake that nearly crushed my knuckles. He had a full black beard and wore dark blue overalls and a woolen stocking cap.

"Glad you decided to join us. Where are you from?"

I gave him a brief summary.

"Are you hungry?"

"Hungry is my middle name." I gladly accepted his offer of brown beans, salted herring and French bread, a typical underground meal I soon found out. While I ate, the bearded giant explained where I was, but not knowing Paris that well, I still wasn't too sure.

"We have a job tonight, so you'll need to get some sleep. Claim a bed upstairs. Several other fellows are already up there resting." He showed me to a closet and pulled down a ladder. "In the meantime I'll get you some coveralls."

In the loft I found five men spread out on the floor, all asleep but one.

"Bon jour," he said.

"Bon jour."

"There are beds in the corner."

The beds were unlike any I'd ever seen. I found a spot and set up the two foot square frame with a piece of canvas stretched over it. One end had a stand to lift it three to four inches off the floor. I noticed how the other underground members rested their heads and shoulders on the canvas, leaving the rest of their bodies sprawled on the floor. I copied them. It was not easy to fall asleep. I had not adjusted to a nighttime work schedule nor to the bed. But finally sleep overtook me and I woke to see stars appear through the slanted window in the ceiling. "The giant" arrived with a pair of coveralls, gym shoes and underwear and said I could take a bath downstairs. The bath and change of clothes made me feel like a million bucks.

As we sat around the table after dinner, one of the men brought out candles and cork and started burning it to make blacking for our faces.

"Tonight we're going headhunting," one of the younger underground men informed me as he dabbed charred cork on his cheeks and forehead. After darkening our faces, we left the house and in the light of a near-quarter moon, followed one another to a country road in a forest at the edge of the city. Crouching silently, we hid in the woods to make sure all was clear.

When the leader gave the signal, one of the men unrolled some wire. The fellow beside me said, "Take this and run across the road." He handed me the wire. "I'll be there to help you." By the time I had the wire straightened out he'd arrived. He pointed to the mark on his sleeve at the shoulder. "Mark your sleeve at this height," he said handing me a piece of chalk. We then anchored the wire at both ends at the right height and angle. No one had explained the trap to me but I was getting the picture. Two men stayed at either end of the wire and the rest of us split up to hide along the sides of the road.

My self-appointed guide whispered, "I'll bet you a cigarette that the motorcycle messenger will fly at least that far," he said and pointed ten feet down the road.

That's a long way for a headless man to go, I thought, without taking my guide up on his bet. I figured he'd had more experience at this thing than I had.

"It could get dangerous," he continued, "because some cycles are equipped with a bar in front of the handlebars to deflect the wire. Then one of the men with a bayonet will finish him off." I think he sensationalized the sabotage to show he was the professional and I the newcomer.

No motorcycle messengers passed that night, so no important messages were intercepted. The next night we had better luck at a different location. After setting up, we'd waited about two hours before I heard an engine in the distance.

I whispered to the young man next to me, "What if it's a truck?"

"Not a problem. It will break the wire and we'll just have to put up another one."

In a minute we could see the motorcycle approach. Everyone tensed in preparation. We had set up on a straight stretch of road, hoping the driver couldn't resist gunning the motor. According the plan the soldier accelerated on the straightaway. One resistance fighter waited at the end of the wire, three down the road, and I stood ten feet behind the wire with a shovel in my hand. My heart thudded as those final seconds ticked by. I'd been told my job was to, "Bury any part that gets cut off."

What I'd expected, happened. In the moonlight I watched the wire sever the German soldier's head. I chased the rolling helmet down the road. The driverless motorcycle crashed onto its side. I grabbed the helmet and blood spurted all over me. For a moment I felt like a spectator at a movie. This couldn't be happening to me! I snapped back to reality, quickly dug a hole and buried the driver's head. The Nazis had taught me well—life is cheap. But I wasn't sure I'd ever get used to the idea. I looked to see if the men burying his body needed any help. They didn't. One of our men drove off on the motorcycle and another took down the wire. We left carrying the satchel of messages. I never learned what those messages said. Later I found out that the motorcycle had been driven to the barn of a farmer and hidden in his hay for the use of the underground.

When we arrived at our hide-out that morning, a face unfamiliar to me awaited us. Guillaume, a short stocky Frenchman with a droopy mustache, had just returned from Switzerland where he'd guided allied pilots downed over France. From there they were airlifted back to England to fly more missions.

Over breakfast he explained his mission and asked me about my background.

"You're just the man I'm looking for," said Guillaume. "I could use a man with your travel experiences and skill with languages. I'd like you to come on my next trip to learn the route and meet my contacts. I'm not sure how many more of these trips I have left in me and I'd like to start training a new man."

I preferred travel to decapitating motorcycle messengers, so agreed to take the job. I'd regained a lot of strength in the month since escaping Buchenwald so thought I could handle it. With only a few hours of rest Guillaume and I drove to Versailles, a few miles west of Paris.

After we'd arrived Guillaume introduced me to the organizer of the evacuation. He informed us, "There are two British pilots and one American pilot to take out. You can meet them here tomorrow night."

On our drive back to Paris, Guillaume prepared me for my first trip. "Get a good rest. I'll leave it to you to arrange for our provisions for the first three days. Talk to 'the giant.' After that we can replenish our supplies at my contacts along the route."

The next evening at Versailles, Guillaume and I met the three pilots. We shook hands all around and Guillaume took control.

"I put my life in danger the same as you do when you bomb the Germans," he said in good English. "On this trip I'm in command, regardless of whether you are a colonel, a major, or whatever. What I say goes. Clear?"

The captain and two majors agreed wholeheartedly.

Guillaume introduced me as his assistant. Then, while the pilots removed dogtags and anything noisy or reflective, Guillaume showed me the map.

"One more thing before we start out," said Guillaume to the assembled group. "When I make this sound," he made a loud click with his tongue, "dive for the ditch. Danger is near."

"My assistant will take up the rear. When he clicks, the same thing goes."

"I can't click that loud. But I can make a duck call." I demonstrated.

"All right, a duck call then," said Guillaume, smiling and shaking his head.

Water and rations were divided up, and off we started on a ten-to-twelve-day, 260-mile trek to Neuchâtel, Switzerland.

CHAPTER XII

Evacuation to Neuchâtel

THAT FIRST NIGHT we pushed hard and covered thirty miles. "Keep track of landmarks," Guillaume told me as we left. This was difficult, as he stayed away from main roads used by the German military. In the first hour Guillaume tested our response to his click. We dove for the ditch and lay there motionless.

"Good," he said, getting up. "You passed your test."

For a short man Guillaume sure could stride out. He moved for hours without a break. The tall, well-muscled American Major seemed fit, and I didn't have to urge him on. But the lean British Major and the chubby British Captain had trouble keeping up with Guillaume's pace. As I looked around to keep track of landmarks, I noticed the beautiful sky with the moon in its first quarter.

When we finally did take a break, Guillaume combined it with an astronomy lesson. "Look at the moon. If you can make a 'p' out of the moon's sliver that is for 'premier.' meaning first quarter. If you can make a 'd' that is for 'dernier,' meaning last quarter. The majors and the captain were interested in learning more French, but Guillaume insisted on speaking only English. He wanted to develop trust between us and the pilots and felt speaking their language would help.

As the sun rose the next morning, we stopped to eat a breakfast of bread, water and rations stolen by the underground from warehouses the Germans had taken over in Paris. I chuckled at the irony when I noticed the Holland label on my can of applesauce. The Dutch gun I had lifted from the German soldier in the restaurant and now cans of fruit and vegetables were back with their rightful owners. Compared with the trip I had taken from Germany to France after escaping Buchenwald, this was turning into a joy ride.

"We need to go on for a ways," said Guillaume after breakfast. "There's a haystack nearby where we can rest." Three hours later we reached that haystack.

"I'll take the first watch," Guillaume said. "Then each of you will take a two-hour shift."

The rest of us snuggled into the haystack and fell asleep instantly. By evening we were on the go, and again Guillaume pushed us hard. After the third night we stopped at a farm house about six miles outside of Troyes.

An elderly French farmer and his wife whisked us inside before greeting us. They led us to their large cozy kitchen and sat us down at a family-sized table. As if she often fixed breakfast for boarding house guests, the farmer's wife stirred the fire, added more wood and soon served us a frying pan full of eggs. It was such a treat to eat fresh food that I didn't quit until I'd finished a half dozen eggs and downed three frothing glasses of milk.

While his wife cleaned up after breakfast, the farmer ushered the five of us into a closet, up a ladder and into a loft. The floor had been covered with mattresses. We slept like lazy dogs during the day while the farmers carried on their routine chores.

Toward evening, one by one, we came down to take baths. This was no easy task as we had to drag the tub from the back porch into the kitchen, prime the pump at the sink to fill a large kettle and heat the water on the stove. The water heating part of the process was repeated five times. When my turn came to bathe I had time to lie back and study the flowered wallpaper and blue checkered table cloth of this homey kitchen.

We gathered around the wooden table at dinner time and feasted on meat, potatoes and gravy. I hadn't seen that much meat in one place since before the occupation of The Netherlands.

Later Guillaume told me, "On the way back we'll help him slaughter a cow. You realize what a risk they're taking, don't you?"

I nodded.

He explained anyway. "No farmer can slaughter a cow without getting permission from the Germans. If caught, he could be sent to a concentration camp or be shot.

"It was the same in Holland," I told him. Guillaume's strong message made me even more appreciative of the risks these farmers and other French citizens were taking for our survival.

We headed east that night, well rested and supplied with fresh food. Our travels went smoothly, except for one scare. Guillaume clicked his tongue sending us all for the ditch. In the distance the purr of a motorcycle engine sounded. Guillaume must have smelled it, because none of the rest of us heard it until we were face down in the ditch. The sound came closer and finally we could see the German soldier, moonlight glinting off his steel helmet, a rifle slung across his back. I never got over the fear of seeing a uniformed, armed German soldier, a sight that always sent shivers down my spine.

After the soldier passed, Guillaume stood. "He will be taken care of by our Paris friends."

Guillaume led on and by morning we'd reached another hiding place. We ate breakfast and took turns standing watch. That day we slept in our shoes, in case we needed to run from a German patrol. Time passed quickly, since I'd gotten used to sleeping during the day.

"The old man," as we fondly called Guillaume started us out earlier than usual that evening. He seemed tireless. By this time he'd told us that he'd fought in World War I and knew this part of the country like the palm of his hand. "But stay back," he warned, "in case I run into a trap." He got us through another night without any problem and we stopped in a grove of trees. "We are close to Chaumont, about 160 miles from Paris. This is past the half-way point."

It started to rain, but the trees protected us. Drizzle continued to fall as we trekked out that evening. The night went uneventfully and under the still black sky we arrived at a farm house between Chaumont and Vesoul.

A tall French farmer with a bushy mustache invited us in. We followed him as he limped into the kitchen. The mouthwatering smell of simmering stew came from a large black kettle on the wood stove. I wondered why stew was cooking before daybreak, what had caused the farmer's limp, and what had happened to his wife.

"Take a seat," he said in English heavy with a French accent. After setting out plates, he served us hot biscuits and gravy, then joined us at the table.

Rubbing a work-worn hand along his corduroy pants the farmer slowly answered my unasked questions. "In World War I, I got shot in the leg and the doctor had to amputate it. At least I got to come back to my wife and family. Then in this war I lost my wife. One day she went to work in the field and never came back." He paused, took a deep breath and struggled for control. I looked up at his leathery face and into his dark eyes and saw the deep pain there.

He continued. "It was sunset. I got worried and went to look for her. Late that night I found her lying in a field. She'd been shot and killed by a German soldier." He put his rough cracked hands over his face and did not speak for a while.

We finished our meal in silence.

The farmer rose from the table and pointed to the kettle. "Anytime you are hungry, help yourself to the stew. But make sure there is no more than one dish on the table. The German soldiers around here drop in often and they know I am alone." He took us to the adjoining room. "Lift up the rug."

Underneath the rug was a trap door. We climbed down a ladder that led to the basement. The five of us each claimed a bunk and fell asleep immediately. About six hours later I awoke needing to go to the outhouse. On my way back through the kitchen, the aroma of stew drew me to the stove and I helped myself to two heaping bowls. Remembering his warning about the dishes, I rinsed the bowl and spoon and left them in the sink. Before returning to the basement, I looked outside and saw the farmer hobbling as fast as he could from the barn.

He pushed open the door and called in, "There are several German soldiers patrolling the area."

I scurried to the basement and heard the farmer overhead straighten out the throw rug and rearrange the furniture. I woke everyone up. "German soldiers are near. Be ready to hold your breath if necessary."

We all sat quietly on the edges of our bunks listening intently. Not long after, we heard the heavy thump of combat boots on the wood kitchen floor. It sounded like at least four soldiers had arrived. Soon the scuffling of boots and the scraping of the chairs quieted down. We looked at each other, almost afraid to breathe. The American Major pantomimed the soldiers eating greedily, then his expression changed to dismay at finding the pot empty.

Half an hour later the sliding of chairs told us they had finished their meal. I expected the Germans to leave, but then heard the thud of combat boots stomping all over the house. A soldier stopped on the throw rug above our heads. I pinched my eyes closed and held my breath until he moved on. The inspection, sounding like a stampede, lasted another fifteen minutes. Then we heard the front door close and the start-up of a truck engine. I took a deep breath and let the air out in an explosion. Five minutes later the farmer let us out, but hobbled back to the window to make sure the soldiers hadn't tricked him and returned.

When it was safe we went to the kitchen. The American major checked the stew pot. "What did I tell you?" he asked, and smiled his infectious grin.

I'd eaten just in time.

"They come here quite often," said the farmer. "I give them meat sometimes so they'll leave me alone." He went to the barn and returned with more meat and soon had cooked another meal. I had no difficulty eating again. We gathered around the table.

"With those German soldiers around we'll have to be extra careful tonight," said Guillaume, "in case they were suspicious. The moon is fuller now and we'll have to watch our shadows."

After dinner Guillaume motioned for me to come outside. I followed him into the shadow of the barn. He must have used all his senses, including a sixth sense, to make his determination. He finally nodded that everything was all right.

We left about ten minutes later loaded down with a new supply of food. I made sure to note the direction and landmarks. After a long night of walking country roads we ended up near a grove of trees. "That's enough for this night," said Guillaume.

During my watch I wondered if any of my family members were looking into this same sparkling summer sky. I wished we'd had time to make a constellation our link to one another.

The next night Guillaume stopped early. "We're approaching Vesoul and I don't want to get too close to town. Besides, we're less than one hundred miles from the Swiss border and more patrols are out."

The following night we passed Vesoul on the south side and made good time through the night. The two British officers had begun to wear down, especially the pudgy one who'd developed a blister which Guillaume had skillfully treated. The American Major had held up well, and through it all had not lost his smile. Two nights later we arrived outside Neuchâtel.

"We need to get into town around midnight," Guillaume said. "So we'll stay this day and go in tonight." Almost to safety now, I could feel the restlessness of the pilots to finish the trip. But no one questioned Guillaume's decision.

That night Guillaume stopped us at the edge of town. "Come with me," he said, nodding to me. "The rest of you wait here."

We walked into town and down several blocks to a two-story house. Guillaume rapped quickly three times, waited and repeated the code three more times. In half a minute a Frenchman in pajamas and a robe opened the door.

"We have three pilots," said Guillaume.

"Bring them in."

While Guillaume returned to get the pilots, the Frenchman, Marcell, invited me into his living room and offered me a glass of cognac. "To another successful rescue," he toasted.

"To my first successful rescue," I added.

When Guillaume brought the three pilots in, our host served not just a midnight snack, but a banquet. Soon after, Guillaume said his good-byes, a signal to me the time had come to leave our charges in Marcel's capable hands. The British Major and Captain shook my hand and the American grabbed me in a bear hug. "I'll never forget you. My name is Wayne." We never used our real names, but it somehow felt satisfying to put a name with his face.

Minutes later Guillaume and I headed for Paris. We reversed our stops on the return trip. The widowed farmer wanted us to stay longer, but after the previous close call with the German soldiers, Guillaume and I agreed one night would be enough.

The first farmer and his wife convinced us to stay for three days. What a relaxed change of pace. Guillaume and I used it to its fullest. For minutes at a time I could forget that a war raged on as I milked the cows, fed the chickens and helped slaughter a steer. I'd eaten so well on the road that I felt my weight had gone up to 145 pounds.

With more time to think, and the farmer and his wife to remind me of my parents, my family was often on my mind. It was August of 1943. Nearly a year had passed since that fateful day last September at Scheveningen prison when I'd last seen Ma and Pa. Ever since my escape from Buchenwald I'd tried to figure out a way to make contact with them. The Germans censored all mail and monitored all phone calls. For now I'd have to be content with sending mental messages. I'd think positive thoughts and hope our work in the Paris underground paid off and that France and the rest of Europe would eventually be liberated.

One day at a time. That's as far as I could plan.

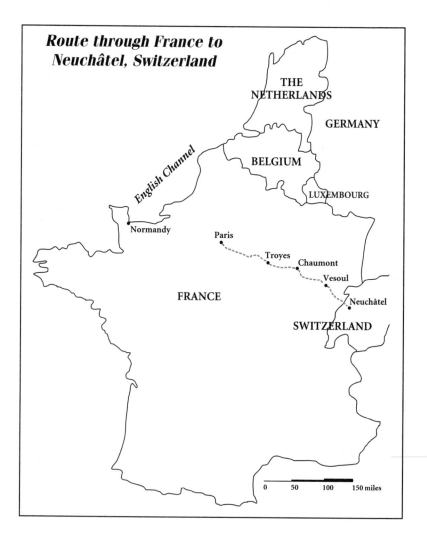

CHAPTER XIII

Leading Solo

AFTER THREE AND A HALF WEEKS away from Paris I found city life about the same. In the interim between trips, I helped break into a government building to steal ID cards and food ration cards for Jews and dissenters who had gone into hiding.

A week later Guillaume came to me. "The underground has picked up several flyers who need passage to the Swiss border. Can you take them alone? I don't feel very good and need to see a doctor."

"I can do it." I felt sorry for the old Frenchman, though my stomach knotted at the thought of the huge responsibility I'd carry on my shoulders. I kept those thoughts inside.

An underground member drove me and the supplies and rations for five to Versailles, the city where Guillaume and I had met the pilots the first time. I was introduced to the four men and shook hands all around.

To set the tone for the trip, I led off with my version of Guillaume's opening speech—"I put my life in danger..., I'm in command regardless of whether you are..." etc.

"It's nice to hear someone speaking English," said a Canadian pilot.

"If everything goes well you will be back with your own troops in England soon," I assured them with more confidence than I felt.

Once food, water, rations and medical supplies had been divided, we hoisted our packs and set off on the opening thirty mile leg of our journey. Within the hour I had them practice diving into the ditch at the sound of my duck call. The first three days went without a hitch, and we arrived safely at the stop-over with the French farmer and his wife.

After having spent three days with them on Guillaume's and my return trip, they greeted me like a family member. In private they asked about Guillaume and expressed sorrow at his ill health.

"Guillaume and I go way back," said the farmer. "We fought side by side in World War I."

That night when the farmer's wife set a huge platter of meat on the table, one of the Americans stared at it in amazement. "This sure beats the hell out of C-rations," he said grinning and served himself.

I was extra careful about following Guillaume's directions, so it took me a day longer to get from the first farm to the tall widower's farm. Nevertheless I felt proud to have led the four pilots safely this far. En route I'd told them about the unannounced visit of the German soldiers on my previous trip.

The talkative American quipped, "Let us know when you go for the stew, so we don't lose out."

We'd reached safety in the widower's warm kitchen and had enjoyed a day of uninterrupted rest. Now we sat around the table savoring an evening meal before departure.

"Without a doubt you make the tastiest stew I've ever eaten," I said to the farmer. Overcome by the tantalizing aroma and flavor, I thought of the starving prisoners in Buchenwald. They'd probably forgotten that such good food existed.

"It's the best way I know of to prepare for your group and for the German soldiers who drop in." replied the farmer modestly.

"Have you had more soldiers come by?" I asked.

"Last week two were here on a motorcycle with a sidecar."

"Do you think they suspect this route is being used to transport allies to Switzerland?"

"No. I think they were just hungry," the farmer assured me.

"Both were older and didn't seem to be SS or fanatic Nazi troopers."

"The only good German soldier is a dead one," I commented. I knew in my heart that this was not true. But I still carried such hatred for the Nazis who ran Buchenwald that it was hard to see beyond their brutality.

The French farmer smiled.

That night we headed out again. For the rest of the trek it seemed like the Lord had sent a guardian angel to ride on my shoulder. Without incident I got the four pilots to Neuchatel and delivered them to Marcel.

On my way back to Paris I stayed longer with the widowed farmer. This time we sat up late into the night and he shared some of his World War I experiences.

"In World War I, we had to wear gas masks a lot because we never knew when the Germans would use poison gas." Shifting his artificial leg to a more comfortable position he continued. "I remember the early tanks and planes. They weren't nearly as powerful as those in the second World War. . . . Back then we fought a lot of man-to-man combat. I saw a Frenchman and a German in a bayonet battle. They struck each other at the same time. They stood balanced, both dead."

I told him about my experiences in Buchenwald and he asked a lot of questions about the details of my escape.

"Your story is so interesting," he explained, "because since France was defeated, I've had several friends sent to different camps in Germany." His eyes held a faraway look. "I've often wondered if there was any chance they would escape."

"Not much chance," I answered honestly. "Do you have any children?" I asked to change the subject. I looked around for family photos and not seeing any figured he must have hidden them from the prying eyes of the German soldiers.

Tears came to his eyes, and he cleared his throat. "I had one son who fought in the French Army. On Christmas Day in '39 he was on the Maginot line. The French and German soldiers came out of their foxholes to toast Christmas. When my son walked back to his trench he stepped on a mine and was killed."

I sat motionless, unable to speak. Both his son and his wife had died within a short time. He must be lonely. No wonder he welcomed our visits. He insisted I stay longer and I did. When I left he gave me some underwear, socks, and shoes that had belonged to his son, and a backpack full of food and drinks.

The first farmer on our route and his wife also insisted I stay for a few days. I left there a couple of pounds heavier and carrying a package for Guillaume. When I got back to Paris, I inquired about Guillaume.

"Guillaume is still sick and staying at someone's house," a fellow underground member told me. He planned to visit Guillaume so I sent the package with him.

About a week later I again headed for Neuchâtel, this time with three British pilots. That trip became distinctive for the discussions of royal families. These pilots of the Royal Air Force argued staunchly for their King and other royalty.

"I have to admit that I'm an anti-royalist," I told them. "I'll fight for my country, but not for our Queen."

"I'd gladly give my life for King George VI," said one pilot.

Despite our disagreements about royalty, we parted the best of friends in Neuchâtel.

"If you ever get to England, look us up, old chap," one of them offered. "We'd welcome you to our homes." I wished then and at the end of every trip that I could have written down names and addresses, but it would have been too dangerous for everyone involved for me to carry such information in my pocket.

Even though the weather had gotten colder, my fourth trip to Neuchâtel was very enjoyable, made so by the three Americans I escorted out of France. The Texan, I knew from our first meeting, would be a real character. I called him "Tex." He called me "Dutch." He carried a long sheath knife strapped to his leg, and boy did he know how to use it. The South Carolinian never missed a chance to brag about southern fried chicken, and the third crew member, from California, talked constantly about the movie stars he'd met and the glamorous life in his home state.

I guessed that none of them had experienced any true hardships in their lives until they'd been shot down north of Paris. All were in the same plane, the pilot, navigator and bombardier, and upon parachuting to earth had landed far apart. It had taken more than a week for them to be reunited after the French underground picked them up.

Along the route, when I felt it was safe, Tex practiced his knife throwing skills. He was damned good. He'd give me pointers and let me make a few throws. The knife had such good balance that before long my throwing improved greatly.

This trip went uneventfully except for one jump into the ditch when I'd spotted a German patrol. I delivered the Americans to the border town of Neuchâtel, none the worse for wear.

As I was about to leave, Tex said, "Dutch." He unstrapped the knife sheath from his leg. "I want you to have this. You are as good with it as I am."

"Thanks a lot, Tex," I said, taking it. "I know how much you value this knife."

"If you ever get to Texas, look me up," said Tex. "You are welcome at my house any time. Thanks for everything, and God bless you." As we shook hands, the South Carolinian and Californian also thanked me profusely.

Tex's knife gave me great comfort as I traveled alone through the nights back to Paris. When I had returned, the first thing on my agenda was to find Guillaume. I'd missed him and wanted to share my travel adventures with him. But no one could tell me where he was or how to find him. I never heard from him again.

One evening in the attic of the house of the Paris underground, an older man came to me. "Would you like to join the French Foreign Legion? It would get you out of here and off to Morocco."

"Who is going?"

"Many French boys and some German deserters," he answered.

"I'm not interested," I said, not revealing that I could never serve side-by-side with a German. A couple of days later I noticed that several faithful members of the underground were gone.

It was coming up on Christmas of 1943. Even though there were no celebrations, it still was one hell of an improvement over my previous Christmas spent in "The Hole." I had regained my health. Now if I could only find out about my family.

After the first of the year there were again flyers to take to the border—an American and a Canadian. I'd packed extra clothes to keep us warm. The trip went smoothly until the last leg between Vesoul and Neuchâtel.

I heard a motorcycle and made my duck call. The Canadian and I dove into the left ditch and the American into the right one. As the motorcycle drew nearer I could tell it moved more slowly than usual. Finally we saw the slit of light from the head beam, but also a second light. The soldier trained a flashlight into the right ditch. Fear gnawed at my stomach. Our route had been discovered! I lay as quietly as I had while faking death on the body pile at Buchenwald.

As the German soldier approached, he slowed even more. He must have heard something or seen a movement. Because of the engine's noise I could draw out my knife without being detected. I waited, covered in a cold sweat, for his next move.

The soldier stopped his motorcycle, got off and kicked down the stand. In one motion he took the machine gun off his back and aimed it at the American crouched in the ditch.

The American stood slowly, his hands raised above his head.

Instinctively I cocked back my arm and with all my strength threw the knife between the German's shoulder blades.

Thunk. The soldier froze in his tracks for an instant.

I thought he might still shoot the American, then turn the gun on us.

In slow motion, the soldier dropped his gun and crumpled to the ground.

The Canadian sprinted to the fallen German, grabbed his gun and pointed it at him. By this time the American had joined him. He checked the German's pulse and nodded that the soldier was dead. He turned to me, an astonished look on his face. "Where in hell did you learn to throw a knife like that?"

Now that my heartbeat had almost returned to normal I could speak. "From a Texan," I told him. "And by the way, I'd like my knife back."

The American pulled the knife from the soldiers back, cleaned it on his pant leg and handed it to me. "Thanks, pal." he said.

Now we had another problem—what to do with the body and the motorcycle. We pulled everything off the road and far into a farmer's field, then waited until daylight. I checked the body for papers, food and money. The pilots took everything of value for souvenirs and I took the French and German money.

In the dawn's light I saw a farmhouse a mile and a half away. After finding a hiding place for the pilots, the soldier's body and the motorcycle I carefully crossed the field to the house. A young fellow of about fifteen ran out.

"Where is your father?" I asked.

"In the house," he answered and turned to go inside.

When the young man returned with his father, the farmer stared at me suspiciously. I had no choice but to trust him, so explained what had happened. "Do you have a shovel we could borrow?"

The farmer got the shovel. "My son and I will bring a wagon to pick up the motorcycle."

I recrossed the field and returned to the waiting pilots. We took turns digging the hole, pushed the body in, filled the hole and packed down the earth. To cover our tracks and those made by dragging the body and motorcycle, we cut tree branches and scratched out all sign that we had been there.

Just before dark the farmer and his son arrived with their horse-drawn wagon piled high with straw. It took all of us to lift the bulky motorcycle into the wagon, then we covered it with straw.

Soon the pilots and I were on our way.

"If we could have used the cycle," said the Canadian, wishfully, "we could have reached our destination by now."

As we walked I noticed a bulge under the coat of the American. When I felt it, I knew he'd taken the machine gun.

"It's not a good idea to carry a German weapon. We'll ditch it in the next culvert."

We arrived safely in Neuchâtel and I turned the pilots over to Marcel. I wondered how he got them back to England, but for confidence sake knew I shouldn't ask.

On my trip back from Neuchâtel I checked the field where we'd buried the German soldier and could see no sign of disturbance. I wondered if the military had sent out a search party to find their missing comrade. I was afraid this incident might indicate a larger problem.

Had the Germans figured out our escape route?

CHAPTER XIV

Last Mission

WHILE RECUPERATING IN PARIS I thought about all the miles I'd walked, but at least while on the road I was well fed. City radios and newspapers bombarded me with depressing war news. According to the propaganda, the Germans were winning on all fronts. Over the radio they sang songs such as, *Wir fahren gegen Engeland,* "we'll travel toward England." The roar of American and British bombers flying overhead made sweeter music to my ears.

I didn't know why, but while in Paris I had frequent nightmares about being confined in "The Hole," about the experiments I'd done as a doctor, and about lying among dead bodies. I'd wake up sweating and thrashing about on my makeshift bed. My fellow underground workers told me I'd cry out as if being tortured. Breaking up their sleep caused some irritability in an already tense situation.

I was relieved to get notice that another group of five pilots needed guidance to Switzerland. After the close call with the German motorcycle soldier I felt a little nervous, although I did not let on. At our rendezvous point in Versailles, one of the pilots rushed over and greeted me like a long lost friend. In the dim light I took a good look at him and realized he was Wayne from my first trip out with Guillaume.

"What are you doing back here?" I asked, slapping him on the back.

"Must be destiny," he answered. "I got shot down in almost the same place. As I parachuted down I thought of seeing you and Guillaume again. Where is he?"

"I haven't seen him for several months and nobody seems to know where he is. He may have been picked up by the Gestapo."

"That would be a damned shame," said Wayne.

I gathered everyone together. "I'll be your tour guide this trip." Three American and two British pilots made up this group.

"During this crossing we'll have to be very cautious," I said. "On recent trips we've had more run-ins with German soldiers. The Germans may have extra troops patrolling the area, so we'll travel off the roads and keep our eyes and ears open."

"Will we make the same stops?" asked Wayne.

"Yes. By now I can practically get you there blindfolded."

Wayne stayed at my side almost the whole trip. He asked questions about my life and told me a lot about himself and the United States.

"What run-ins with German soldiers have you had lately?" he asked. "I remember clear as day hearing the German soldiers tromping on the floor above us at the widower farmer's house."

I told him about how on our last trip we'd killed and buried a German soldier and left the motorcycle with a farmer and his son to hide in their barn.

"I hope your luck isn't running out." Wayne paused as if unsure whether to ask a question. Slowly he went on, "Dutch, why don't you come back with us to England? We could use an interpreter like you."

"That would be unfair to the resistance fighters," I said, "especially when I couldn't even let them know. Anyway I don't have any contacts in England."

"I could take you to the American Headquarters and introduce you to someone who'd be very glad to meet you."

"But that doesn't take care of my concern about notifying the French underground. And, what if you got shot down a third time?"

"Another underground member would get me out, or by then I could find the border on my own," he said grinning. "And I'm sure someone could get your message through to the Paris underground."

Wayne had given me a lot to think about. As I lay on watch staring into the sky, I tried to picture what the next step in my life would be. *Wayne seems to be very sincere. I think he would help me.*

Wayne and I talked about it every day. The other two Americans became involved and encouraged me to come to England. By the time we'd reached the Swiss border, I had decided to leave with them. With this change in plans, I wondered again about my family. It had been one and a half years since we'd last been together. Maybe from England I'd have a better chance of contacting them.

This trip went smoothly, although I moved with extreme care through the territory where we'd met up with the German soldier on the motorcycle.

When our group arrived in Neuchâtel, I followed the same knocking procedure on Marcel's door. He again answered the door in his pajamas and robe.

"I have five pilots and a civilian."

Mon Dieu, "My God," said Marcel.

"Where is the civilian?" asked Marcel after I brought back the rest of the pilots.

"You are looking at him," I replied.

"You're finally getting smart. Are you staying in Switzerland or going on to England?"

"To England. Do you think there are too many of us?"

"They can take just three at a time, so we'll do it in two trips."

What "it" was, I wasn't sure. I'd never been told anything specific about how pilots were transported back to England from Neuchâtel.

Marcel left with a flashlight and came back an hour later. "Captain will be here in an hour and a half."

When the Captain arrived, the large full-bearded man inspired respect just by stepping into a room. He reminded me a lot of "the giant," leader in the Paris underground. Though he was quiet compared to the friendly, talkative giant. Only when we'd finished eating and the Captain had sipped the last drop of his cognac did he speak. "Who will go first?" he asked in a rumbling voice.

Wayne wanted to stay with me. I suggested, "Take the two Englishmen and one American tonight and the rest of us tomorrow night."

The Captain and three pilots left immediately.

The next day, as our departure time grew nearer, I felt more and more excited about going to England. *Maybe this is the time to quit the underground before my luck does run out,* I thought. Marcel agreed to notify the Paris underground of my departure. Captain returned that evening for dinner and his pre-journey cognac.

"How did last night's trip go?" I asked.

"No trouble at all," he said. "They should be in Zurich tonight."

I translated this for Wayne. "That's how we did it last time," he said.

Before we left Marcel's house to cross Lake Neuchâtel, Captain gave us instructions. "I need two of you to row and one in front to hit the ice with a metal bar to keep the raft from getting punctured. I'll guide from the back." We followed Captain through the dark cobblestone streets to the lake. Captain pulled the rubber raft out from under some bushes and pushed it into the water.

"Jump in," he whispered.

Wayne and the other American took the oars and paddled as skillfully and quietly as if they did it every night. I held the bar ready, watching in front of the raft like my life depended on it. I'd been told to look out for any suspicious objects, because the Germans had mined the lake sometime back.

Slowly and carefully the Captain guided us across the lake. Soft shadows danced on the water. It was silent except for the gurgle of paddles dipping into the water and the slosh of water against the bow of the raft.

Captain said that we had an ideal night—dark, but not so dark that we couldn't see each other and his signals. About six hours later we pulled the raft from the water on the opposite shore at the feet of a waiting group of people.

I felt like I'd broken loose from an ankle chain. I could have jumped ten feet high. We climbed into the back of a canvas-topped truck. In my excitement I'd forgotten to thank Captain. He stood waving, deep satisfaction written all over his face for another mission completed. I waved my thanks.

As we swayed along country roads Wayne said, "The Swiss have to keep up the appearance of staying neutral, so in Zurich they'll put us up in an out-of-the-way hotel. No embassy this trip."

Peeking out through the slit in the canvas at the back of the truck I could see it was even too early for the cows to be up. Several hours later when we arrived in Zurich we were reunited with the other three pilots.

"We're in luck," said the American whom we could now call Dave. "The pick-up is tonight. Flying over France and the North Sea will still be dangerous, but if we're downed we'll have our own private guide to take us back to the Swiss border."

That evening an official from the British Embassy informed us, "There will be no pick-up tonight. I'll let you know when it is rescheduled. Stay inside as much as possible. You never know where a German spy will turn up."

After having slept on concrete, on wooden platforms, and in open fields, I didn't mind the extra day resting on a real bed. That evening we were told to prepare for pick-up that night. After dinner I found a current newspaper and caught up on the latest news, the same old story—the Germans were winning on all fronts. Things still looked hopeless for the Allies.

Wayne signaled me to come to a meeting room. To my surprise, twenty people waited there. Several came from the British and

American Embassies, but the rest were downed pilots or dissenters awaiting airlift to England. It wasn't until then that I realized the French underground used several routes to get people out of France. This knowledge made me feel better about leaving the Paris underground on such short notice.

An embassy official stood, and the already quiet room grew quieter. "I'll divide you into groups and assign a driver. You will be taken at intervals to the runway, so everyone will be there by 1:00 A.M."

The plan went like clockwork, and the groups met at the airport to wait for our flight. Before long we heard the drone of a plane's engines and as it drew nearer I felt the crowd shifting around anxiously. Unexpectedly the plane flew over. We stood silently staring at the sky. One of the drivers ran to the main terminal and returned with the news that the plane couldn't pick us up that night. The group groaned in disappointment. I felt restless. *How much longer will we have to wait to get out?* I asked myself. We never found out why the plane didn't land.

Right after breakfast the next morning, as if to make up for the flight delay, we were picked up and driven to St. Moritz ski area. I guess the officials thought we'd be safe there from German spies.

"Do you know how to ski? asked Wayne as we rode up on the bus.

"I water skied, a long time ago. But, I'm not dressed to snow ski."

"Don't worry, they'll fix you up."

They certainly did. I had a wonderful day. After an awkward beginning, I took to skiing like I'd done it for years. For me that day didn't last long enough.

That night we again arrived at the airport by 1:00 A.M. This time the plane landed. In the darkness it looked like a DC-3. As we lifted off for England a tingle ran down my spine: my escape from Buchenwald, my six missions to Neuchatel, my decision to leave for England, and yesterday's schussing down the mountain left me feeling exhilarated.

What's in store for me now? I wondered. I closed my eyes and set-tled back in my seat. *Could it be that the Lord had returned from vacation and was now making up for lost time?*

With the United States 101st Airborne Division
Normandy to the Battle of the Bulge

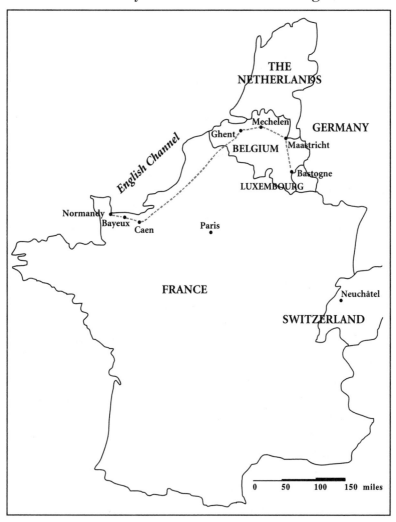

CHAPTER XV

Normandy

A S I RESTED MY HEAD against the seat listening to the drone of the aircraft's engines, I realized that I'd recuperated physically, but not mentally, from my concentration camp experiences. What about all those prisoners who had died, and those still in camps? *God, what did you have in mind for them?* I hadn't figured out the purpose for all that sacrifice and misery.

Early in the morning our plane landed at Upper Heyford military base north of London. Within an hour we were led to headquarters to be interviewed. I was one of the first taken into an office, but without identity or official papers I worried that I'd be unable to prove who I was. Wayne came to my rescue by telling the American Colonel that I had guided him to the Swiss border twice, along with other British and American pilots. He explained that he'd persuaded me to come to England, first to get me away from the Nazis and second because I would make a good interpreter. After following through on his promise to help me, Wayne went back to his squadron and regular duties and gradually we lost track of each other.

Two hours after my interview the Colonel called me back into his office. "How would you like to join the American 101st Airborne Division as an interpreter? You would have to be trained as a paratrooper."

"Yes," I answered without hesitation. Here was my chance to help my people and the French.

For the next several weeks I trained as an infantryman and a paratrooper. I spent many hours on the rifle range and many more hours inside a hangar learning parachute folding and jumping skills.

During my initiation as a paratrooper, an instructor handed me a parachute, saying, "Put this on." I fitted it onto my back and fastened the buckles. "Stand on the barrel under the straps." The instructor's assistants fastened the straps hanging from the ceiling to the rings on my chute at the top of my shoulders. An officer kicked the barrel out from under me to give me the feel of the jolt when a parachute opened. I felt it all right; the too-loose straps almost took my ears off. I never forgot that lesson.

The lesson also taught me to listen carefully to instructions, which carried over when I learned to fold and pack my parachute. "You live or die by how well you pack your chute," the instructor emphasized, as he demonstrated the precise technique.

Days later at the jump tower I took my next training step, and a long one it was—a 300-foot drop to simulate a real jump. As I waited my turn at the base of the tower, I double checked to see that my straps were tightly fastened. Two instructor's assistants hooked me into a harness. As I dangled dry-mouthed, heart beating in my throat, they cranked me to the top of the tower. Before I had time to think, the cable released and I shot through the air until the open chute filled with enough air to slow me and float me to the ground. Another sensation I'd never forget.

Without wasting a minute, they had me and the rest of the new paratroopers jumping from planes. As I stood in the open door to take my first jump, wind screaming in my ears, I wasn't prepared for how tiny objects on the ground looked. I swallowed my heart, and leaped, praying to God that my chute would open.

The weeks of training flew past. By now it was spring of 1944, more than a year since I'd escaped from Buchenwald. Frequently I thought about my family and what might have happened to them. As soon as I could get a pass, I rode the military bus fifty miles to London to see if the Red Cross could help me locate my family.

"I'm sorry," a sympathetic woman told me. "I wish there was something I could do. But since Holland is still occupied by the Germans, there is no way to make contact with your family."

At first I felt angry and helpless, and wanted to yell, "I've already waited too long." I understood why the Red Cross could do nothing for me, but that didn't make it any easier to accept.

While in London I also visited the British, Dutch and American embassies and tried to get official papers verifying that I was Jacobus van der Geest. After several interviews I received unofficial papers until the information could be verified after The Netherlands was liberated.

As I rode the bus through the streets of downtown London, I stared in amazement at block after block of flattened, burned-out buildings that had been bombed by German V-1 and V-2 rockets. Seeing the piles of rubble triggered a flashback of downtown Rotterdam four years ago, when Fred and I had hidden in the entryway of the jewelry store and watched a bomb level the department store across the street. *My God, when will it all end?*

With the intense troop training and the high level meetings going on daily at Heyford military base, an Allied invasion of Europe looked imminent. The only questions were where and when. It seemed like the Germans had gotten stronger since The Netherlands had been occupied. Every night more V-1 and V-2 rockets bombed England, most landing on London. Thank God, no rocket-bombs were dropped on our military base, though not a day went by that London radio and newspapers didn't report deaths and damage caused by the monster bombs. The Allies had beaten the Germans in 1918, but this time I wasn't so sure.

Suddenly, what all the military in England had prepared for started to unfold. The evening of June 5th, General Eisenhower mingled and talked with troops of the 101st Airborne. His face had a serious determined look. The troops he talked with radiated confidence. Not until we of the 101st Airborne had lined up next to our planes in the middle of the night were we told, "This is the invasion of Europe. Our division will parachute out over the coast of France."

We weren't told that Utah Beach, Normandy, was our destination. The command came to board. As our C-47, one of 1200 planes, lifted into the darkness and circled south on this cloudy, damp June 6, 1944, all seventy of us sat deep in thought in our seats along the fuselage. In the semi-darkness I went over every detail of my training. For security I patted my M1 rifle and Colt .45 pistol and ran my fingers over the six hand grenades fastened to my belt. I studied the faces of my fellow paratroopers. I had seen many scared faces in my day, but there was no fear in these faces, just a fierce determination to do the job they were trained to do.

Finally a paratrooper next to me broke the silence. "I can't wait to get to those French girls. Say, Dutch, I'll have to stick with you, in case I need an interpreter."

"When you find a French girl, I don't think you'll want a third party around," I joked back.

The roar of engines filled in the silence that followed during most of the hour long flight to and across the English Channel.

"It's a long way to Tipperary," a paratrooper belted out. The men joined in and the chorus bounced off the metal fuselage. Silence again fell. One by one chins dropped to chests and we caught cat-naps or pretended to. My mind raced in disjointed thought. *How'd I ever end up here?—Would my chute open?—Would this be the last day of my life?*

The jumpmaster's harsh voice startled us into action. "Get ready to jump," he bellowed.

That meant tighten all straps and be ready to line up. The jump-master shoved open the door, letting in the high-pitched whistling wind. My heart banged against my ribs. As I waited my turn to jump, I fussed nervously with my parachute straps, pack and weapons. The jumpmaster stood opposite the door, and with an eagle eye inspected each paratrooper to see that his chute had been packed correctly and all straps tightened. He then made a thumbs-up signal to jump. In quick succession each trooper leaped away from the plane. I came last.

"Good luck, Dutch," said the jumpmaster as I stood in the doorway, my jumpsuit snapping in the wind. His thumb went up.

I plunged into a cloudy early morning sky filled with bubble-topped parachutes. I saw black puffs of smoke, smelled gun powder and heard popping sounds like fireworks below and around me. German guns shot at us like we were sitting ducks at a carnival. In the shoreline haze, dozens of ships converged and troop carriers disgorged thousands of troops onto the beaches. My parachute opened and my descent slowed until I reached twenty-five feet above the ground. Suddenly my chute descended faster than was safe for landing. Looking up I discovered bullet holes shot through the nylon. Quickly I checked below and saw I was almost over a German bunker and approaching fast. I pulled the cords to change directions toward the soft sand—but too late.

With a thud I landed on my rear end on the back edge of a bunker. I felt lucky to be alive. In my last moments of descent I'd seen several paratroopers land and not get up. All this time German soldiers fired a machine gun out of the slot near the top front end of the bunker. Other machine guns fired from bunkers around me.

Furious at seeing my friends die, I became obsessed with revenge. Recklessly I threw off my chute, crept around the corner of the bunker to where I could see the machine gun barrel sticking out of the slot, continuing to rattle away like mad. As I belly-crawled closer to the opening, I reached for a grenade. I pulled the pin letting the clip fly, counted three seconds and hand delivered the grenade through the machine gun slot. I rolled back and flattened out on the ground. An ear shattering blast followed and the machine gun went silent. I waited a moment, and to make sure no one survived threw in a second grenade. I lay there, heart beating wildly, mouth and face gritty with sand. No sound or movement came from the bunker.

A minute later our platoon commander signaled us to advance. "On the double," shouted the tall, muscular Colonel.

We climbed the sand dunes, scooted over a hill, crossed a causeway and moved into the flat countryside all the while under fire from German troops on the run. I wasn't until then that I realized that my tail bone was very sore from my hard landing. As we ran, we took cover from the spray of German gunfire by jumping into existing holes created by mines and bombs. One by one the infantry cleared out German positions in farm houses and fields and continued to advance southeast into France. Being an interpreter for the 1st Battalion, I stayed in the second line of offense and questioned German soldiers as soon as they'd been captured and brought back from the front lines.

Late that day, my left leg started to itch like hell. I sat on my sore rear end in a bomb hole and pulled my pant leg out of my boot. Blood ran down my leg. A blood trail stained my pants from thigh to boot. I felt up and down my pant leg and discovered a hole. Soon a medic arrived, ripped my pants open and examined my leg.

"You've been hit by shrapnel in the back of your thigh. I'll send for help."

I must have lost more blood than he or I thought. Before he was out of sight, I blacked out.

I woke up in a hospital field tent, my leg heavily bandaged.

CHAPTER XVI

Battle to Holland

T HE DOCTOR SAID MY LEG would be fine, and the next day I was able to hobble around. In the following days I had to walk only a few steps to do my job, from the hospital tent to the Bayeux City Hall where headquarters had been set up.

On my first morning back on the job an American intelligence officer called me in to interpret for him. Three captured German soldiers were being held for interrogation and one by one they were led to his office between two American Military Police.

The Major told me to warn each, "You are being held as a prisoner of war. If you lie you'll regret it." After they'd given their name, rank and serial number I asked two questions; "Where did you come from?" and "How many are in your division?" The three prisoners, all scared young infantry soldiers, willingly answered the questions. The MPs took them to a makeshift prison.

"If the prisoners don't cooperate," I said to the Major, "I know some better ways to get answers out of them." From a previous conversation he knew I'd been tortured in a concentration camp.

"I'll keep that in mind," he said. Each word jiggled the cigarette he pinched between his lips, and the straps of his helmet dangled casually, giving him a very unmajor like look.

American, British and Canadian forces fought village by village along the coast eastward from Bayeux. Day and night our intelligence unit heard gunfire and smelled smoke from our vantage point on the second line. Everyday soldier-filled trucks, tanks, and jeeps with machine guns mounted on the front headed for the front line. Stretchers carrying wounded soldiers back from the front line to the field hospital were just as common a sight. After a while I got used to this constant noise and activity and in my exhaustion could even sleep in an open field without hearing anything.

On any day the most beautiful sight to me was watching a group of dejected German soldiers with their hands held over their heads marching back from the front. I knew I had my interrogation work cut out for me, but this was a sign that our troops were making steady progress eastward toward The Netherlands.

French farmers and villagers ran out to greet us as Allied soldiers fought for and regained their freedom and property for them. Overjoyed, they opened their homes to us and offered us whatever was left of their meager supplies.

Finally on June 25th, almost three weeks after the Normandy invasion, the Allies broke out from the beachheads. Between the landing at Normandy and the breakout, our headquarters moved eastward behind the front lines as the territory became secured. In my day-to-day job as an interpreter, I questioned all German prisoners captured in the area. Sometimes I traveled to nearby towns to work for other American commanders.

For a month forward movement stalled in Hermanville, north of the British 6th Airborne landing, until the liberation of Caen. The Germans put up a strong resistance at Caen, which wasn't captured until July 9th. Even so, our troops never wavered in their determination to push the Germans out of France. I walked through Caan after the Germans fled. It could hardly be called a city anymore. Rubble lay in heaps everywhere. Almost every building had been destroyed beyond repair. Here and there a church tower stood up from a crumbling building.

After the fall of Caen, German troops retreated eastward in a complete rout. In their haste they left tanks, armored cars, rations, field tents etc. behind. They tried to destroy most of the heavy equipment. Almost daily our headquarters moved to a different town, through Dieppe, Lille and into Ghent, Belgium. As Allied forces liberated town after town, the local population mobbed the streets. As we approached Belgium, my hopes soared that I'd be part of the forces to liberate The Netherlands.

Late into an early September afternoon, I arrived in Ghent, Belgium, a town already in full swing celebrating its liberation. Less than twenty-four hours earlier the Germans had retreated from Ghent. As I rode down the crowded street in a Jeep driven by an American Captain, children waved flags, and men and women scrambled onto our Jeep hugging and kissing us and offering us toasts. When the Captain saw a friend he knew from the States he pulled over and jumped down to greet him.

"I'm going for a walk," I told the captain, "so just take your time."

In less than half a block I met a soldier from the 3rd Canadian Division. He greeted me in a friendly way and asked about my shoulder patch which read "Interpreter." I explained who I was and what I did.

"I live in Manitoba province,' he said. "We don't speak French there, but in other parts of Canada they do."

"Which town do you live in?"

"A town west of Winnipeg, called Brandon."

"I'm from Holland."

"My grandfather came from there. I have a Dutch name. DeGroot, John DeGroot."

"DeGroot is my mother's maiden name."

We talked for fifteen or twenty minutes more trying to figure out if we were related. We found no connection, but in Holland, DeGroot is a common name.

Yawning John said, "I'm going to get some sleep. He nodded toward a building in front of us. "The Germans used it. There are plenty of beds left."

After wishing him well, I turned back toward the Captain and his friend. I had taken only one step when a huge explosion blew out the windows and door of the building John had entered. The blast threw me to the ground. Unhurt, I jumped up, ran to the doorway and looked inside. John lay there, his right arm and part of his face blown off. *He didn't have a chance. The damned Germans booby-trapped the building.* I squatted beside him, tears streaming down my face. Even though I'd just met him a short time ago, we'd become friends. I'll always remember John. When I looked up, there stood the Captain and his friend beside me.

"Did you know him?" the Captain asked.

"We just met and talked for a while."

The Captain nodded understandingly and pulled me to my feet. "Let's get the hell out of here. There might be more booby-traps planted. I'll call in the bomb squad and have them check the building out."

How close we all are every minute to getting killed, I thought as I slowly walked away. *The poor parents of John DeGroot from Brandon.* John's death reminded me of the death of the tall French widower's son, killed by a mine while walking to his trench— neither had died by direct enemy fire.

The Captain stopped at a building occupied by the Allies and reported the incident. That night I couldn't sleep. The gruesome blast scene kept going through my mind. It was still with me two days later when our forces arrived in Mechelen. I never entered a building in a retaken town before it had been checked out by the bomb squad.

Soon after our arrival the Belgian underground contacted us. "We've picked up all the Nazi collaborators, including the mayor and the girls who went out with German soldiers."

"Your jail must be packed full," I said in Flemish.

"Oh, no. We put them all in the zoo," he said grinning. He proudly took us to the captives. We arrived to find all the monkey cages filled with collaborators, and members of the Belgian underground guarding the traitors. Heads of the girls were shaved, though they tried to cover their shame with scarves. *I hope Rieta, who betrayed our family, gets ten times worse punishment than this,*

I thought. *And I hope my fellow Dutch underground members shaved her head too.*

The Allied troops fought steadily eastward and our intelligence unit moved behind them. Practically every day I interviewed German POWs. Now I did the interrogations on my own. I'd received an official list of questions to ask: How many men are there in your regiment? Where do you come from? Where are your supplies of ammunition and food?

Most of the German soldiers answered the questions willingly, except the hard-core SS troops and Nazis. And I had ways to get the information out of them, the vengeful ways they'd taught me.

Finally our intelligence unit arrived in Maastricht. The Netherlands at last! After four long years I stepped onto the soil of my home country. A current of energy ran from the tips of my toes up my spine to my brain like a shock from an electrical appliance. Maastricht was liberated. I felt liberated. All I could think about was that the Allies would swing north and free all of The Netherlands and I would finally see my family.

The townspeople informed us that the Germans had blown up the bridge across the Maas River, north of town. As I walked the streets, I checked out the remains of the bridge, then turned to walk downtown. I passed a bakery, and the aroma reminded me of my father's bread factory and shop. As if it were a warm flour-dusted hand, the smell of fresh bread beckoned me through the door and up to the counter.

The chubby baker and his thin wife dropped what they were doing and greeted me like a friend.

The baker looked over my American uniform and said in poor English, "Take whatever you like to eat."

"I can speak Dutch," I said in Dutch. Everyone in the shop gathered around asking questions.

"I was born in Holland," I told them, "and after a long journey ended up in England to join the American forces as an interpreter." While standing there I noticed a calendar on the wall. It was Saturday, September 16. In my excitement I blurted out, "Tomorrow is my birthday. I'll be twenty-one years old."

The baker and his wife both asked, "What is your name?"

"Jacobus van der Geest, now Jack."

"Will you be in town tomorrow, Jack?" asked the baker.

"As far as I know, but I can't be sure from day to day."

"Then we'll have a birthday party," said the jovial man. He unbuttoned his tight white baker's coat as if needing more freedom to express his enthusiasm. "Jack, could you be here at twelve o'clock? And bring a friend. Everyone is invited," he called out, waving his arms to include the people in the shop.

That evening I asked the American Captain to come. When he picked me up in a Jeep the next day, he sang, "Happy birthday to you . . ." In the back of the Jeep sat a large carton, but since it was closed I couldn't tell what it contained.

As we pulled up in front of the bakery, the Captain said, "Bring the box in."

The door stood wide open and the baker's wife escorted us to their living room in the back of the store. She'd changed her white baker's dress for a dressier one. I set the box down and introduced the Captain. The baker's wide wife threw her arms around the Captain, saying in Dutch, "You will never know how much we love you people, our heroes, our liberators. You will always be in our prayers."

I translated for him. From then on the baker and his wife spoke their broken English when talking to him.

The Captain opened the box to show the baker and his wife supplies of flour, sugar and other food. "I'm a friend of the cook," he said with a sly smile. Before the exclamations had died down, like a magician he pulled a bottle of French cognac from his coat pocket. "This I took from the Germans who had stolen it from the French. So let's have a party! I haven't been to a party in a long time."

At the height of the party, the room filled with friends and neighbors, the baker dramatically carried in a beautiful cake. Printed in scroll on top was: Happy 21st Birthday, Jack.

I swallowed hard to keep tears from flowing down my face. The baker's wife gave me a big kiss on each embarrassed cheek.

As the party wound down one of the guests said to me, "My wife and I would like to invite you to our apartment after the party. We live about one block down the street on the second floor. Bring your friend."

"Thank you," I said. "We'd like to come."

About three o'clock the celebration broke up. It was a great party and the baker and his wife thanked us again and again for the box of supplies.

We followed the second couple, Arie and his wife, to their apartment. We all sat down on the old but still comfortable furniture.

"We are so happy that we are free,' our hostess said. "And we pray that each one of you will get home safely."

Arie stood, walked to a cabinet and pulled out a bottle of Bols, a Dutch drink. He filled four small liquor glasses and handed one to each of us. "For a very special day, Jack." Arie said. "For liberation, and now that you're twenty-one, for the first day you can drink." He winked, "Prost." We sat drinking and talking for a while.

Soon the Captain and I had to get back on duty.

At the door Arie handed the Captain and me sealed envelopes. "This is a gift from both of us."

"Thank you for everything," I said, "and I can't tell you how happy I am to be back in my home country." I had no idea when he'd filled the envelopes.

In the Jeep we each opened our envelopes and found one hundred guilders, about $30. We sat speechless. At first I felt we should return the money. "That would be an insult," I said after a moments thought. "He wouldn't have given it to us if he couldn't afford it."

"Happy birthday, Jack,' said the Captain, and handed me his envelope. "You can use this better than I can."

"Thanks. It's been an unforgettable birthday."

After checking in at headquarters we drove west to Hasselt where we spent the night. "We need to get to Eindhoven by tomorrow evening," the Captain explained. "While we celebrated your birthday the battle to free The Netherlands started. Early this morning the 101st Airborne landed near Eindhoven, the U.S. 82nd Airborne at Nijmegen and the British 1st Airborne at Arnhem."

I pictured these cities on a map and realized that if they were captured, the liberation of Holland would soon follow. My hopes of seeing my family had been raised so often, I felt as if I was on an emotional roller coaster ride. Did I dare let myself hope?

About 6:00 P.M., we drove through the celebrating crowds in Eindhoven, an already liberated city. Throngs of people swarmed through the streets, tasting an only hours-old freedom they hadn't experienced in nearly four and a half years. Exuberantly they shouted and waved. I wanted to jump down into the crowd and join the revelers, but we were expected at headquarters.

When we arrived, intelligence officers told us that two American platoons were chasing retreating Germans toward Nijmegan. Everyone predicted the German rout would continue. Enthusiastically I questioned Dutch government underground workers to find out what facilities were available to the Allies and to learn what they had found out from German intelligence. Repeatedly they told me that capture of the Arnhem bridge was vital to the success of the mission, and that the Germans had a heavy concentration of troops and equipment there. Two days later, German prisoners verified what I had already learned, adding the locations of tanks, artillery and ammunition dumps and the names and numbers of troop divisions.

Within a few days it became apparent that the Germans would not give up Arnhem easily. After a week of bloody battle the Allies had suffered 17,000 casualties. In the end the Germans held the town, blew up the Arnhem bridge and blocked further advancement into The Netherlands.

Reality hit me like a ton of rubble. *Who knows when or if I'll ever see my family again*, I thought in despair.

After the attack on Arnhem failed, the Allies set up a defense south of the Waal River and north of Nijmegen to contain the Germans. Other Allied forces turned their attack east toward the industrial Ruhr Valley of Germany.

Despite the nagging worry about my family, and the losses at Arnhem, the month I spent in Eindhoven eventually turned into a peaceful time for me. Almost every night the grateful citizens of Eindhoven sponsored dances for the Allied troops at local nightclubs and bars.

One night an American Lieutenant and I caught a Jeep ride to a bar with a dance floor and live music. Girls crowded around, hanging on to us and our every word. I danced every dance. After an awkward beginning, the steps I had learned at Saturday night dances in Rotterdam came back. We lost track of time. At 11:30, the Lieutenant was scheduled for duty at 12:00, we discovered our ride had already left. We grabbed our coats, ran out the door and down the street.

Suddenly I stopped. "This won't work," I panted. "We'll never make it to headquarters in time." I looked around, walked up to a dark house and rapped on the door. A sleepy man in pajamas answered.

"I'm sorry to bother you, but we've been stranded and need to get back to headquarters by midnight," I said in Dutch.

He blinked, looked at our uniforms and grinned. "My wife and I have bicycles you can use." He got the bicycles. We jumped on and tore off down the dark quiet street yelling our thanks over our shoulders. At midnight we skidded to a stop in front of headquarters.

The next day I returned the bicycles, much to the owner's surprise.

The fun ended in late October when the 101st Airborne was ordered to load trucks and Jeeps and proceed south to meet up with Patton's Third Army at Bastogne, Belgium. The 101st fought south through light German resistance. In six weeks we traveled back to Maastricht, then south to Liege and Spa to reach Bastogne in the first week of December 1944.

We arrived in Bastogne by truck, not our usual parachute drop from a plane. I looked over the tailgate at the dreary countryside ravaged by war and cluttered with broken down trucks, tanks and other machinery of war. Town residents greeted us as we rode into the town square. Out of precaution they disappeared quickly. They'd evidently heard about the city of Dinant, which had been recaptured by the Germans several times. They were afraid to celebrate too soon, or afraid of what the Germans would do to them if they cooperated with the Allies. In Bastogne we joined up with the 9th and 10th Armored Divisions who already defended the town.

On that day when we reached Bastogne we were totally unprepared for the welcome Hitler had planned for us.

CHAPTER XVII

Battle of the Bulge

I N BASTOGNE, BELGIUM, as the fall of 1944 pushed into winter, temperatures plunged. It seemed like this winter would be colder than usual. From my first floor office in a city government building I could see City Center Park. A bar I soon became familiar with stood on the corner. Between interrogations I at least had a decent view.

By the time the 101st Airborne reached Bastogne I had interrogated so many German POWs that it had become routine. From my seat behind a table I followed a list of prescribed questions, penciled in answers, and later wrote up reports for my commanding officer. I'd go down the list, asking questions quickly and calmly. I didn't give the prisoners much time to think. I wanted automatic responses. If I repeated a question and received a different answer, that was never good for the prisoner's health.

One day a particularly stubborn SS officer refused to cooperate. "All I have to give is my name, rank and serial number," he insisted.

Though I tried to remain calm on the surface, inside I boiled. I couldn't forget my brutal treatment at the hands of the SS at Buchenwald, my family's mistreatment and my bitter disappointment at not getting back to Holland because of strong German resistance at Arnhem. These frustrations, added to the more recent German atrocities—the murder of ninety-two American prisoners at Malmedy—pushed me beyond my limits. I lost my temper when the SS officer quoted to me the rules of the Geneva Convention as if the Germans had followed them all along.

For the second time I asked him to stand at attention. He refused. I called in the MPs waiting outside the door. "Take off his boots. The best way to do that is to brace one foot in his crotch and pull." After they'd wrestled him to the floor, one soldier held the SS officer down while the other used my technique to take off his boots. The MP handed the SS officer's boots to me.

"Would you like us to leave the room?" he asked.

"Stick around," I said, "you might learn something." Again I ordered the SS officer to, "Stand at attention."

He glared at me.

I jumped up and stomped my boot down hard on his toes. "It seems like he thinks he's the Almighty," I said to the MPs. "Let's treat him that way. Jesus was nailed to the cross. Go get me a hammer and nails and I'll nail his feet to the floor."

The face of the SS officer turned as pale as the old snow in the town square.

"I have been a guest of Adolph Hitler in Buchenwald," I shouted in his face. "Now you are my guest. Would you like some of the same treatment he gave me?"

This time he stood at attention when I asked him to.

"Now, let's go on with the questions." When some of his answers were slow in coming, I told him, "I don't have all day. Now you can stand on one leg for the rest of the interrogation." His answers came a little faster, but it wasn't long before he switched to the other leg. This time I kicked him on the leg he first stood on. "Just a reminder, use that leg only."

The questioning progressed more quickly. Eventually he gave me the answers I looked for, but not before his one leg had been kicked out from under him several times. Finally I finished the questioning, the MPs took him away, and I wrote up my report.

Ten minutes later the MPs returned. "We have another SS officer to bring in. And by the way, that last officer asked for his boots."

"Where he's going, he won't need any boots. If either of you wants the boots, take them."

"No," said one MP, "you keep 'em. You earned 'em."

They brought in the next SS officer. He looked at me defiantly and spit in my face. I turned around to clean my face on my handkerchief, and when I came back around I smashed him in the nose with my fist. I felt the bone crack under my knuckles. He rocked back to catch his balance and covered his bloody nose with his hands.

Both MPs grabbed his arms and held him still.

"I have nothing to tell except my name, rank and serial number," the SS officer said, blood trickling onto his lips.

"Let's start with that," I said, grinning menacingly.

He gave me the information.

"Stand at attention when I talk to you," I ordered.

Instead he ignored me and wiped the blood off his nose with the back of his hand.

From where I stood I could look out the window and see a long concrete wall at the back of the next building. "Tie his hands behind his back," I ordered the MPs. "Take him to the wall in the yard." That wall reminded me of the last position in which I'd seen my father. When we got out to the wall, I forced the SS officer to lean against the wall, take three steps back so he supported his body weight on his bloody broken nose. Then I ordered him to sidestep along the wall while maintaining that position. *Revenge for Pa and Ma,* I

Boots taken from SS Officer

thought. As I had done with the first SS officer, I reminded this one that his countrymen had taught me well at Buchenwald. Finally he broke down and gave me the information I needed. His and the other SS officer's information proved useful to our officers and GIs in the 101st Airborne's defense of Bastogne.

Fighting a war is hell on everyone, I thought. I finished my report and handed it to the messenger to take to the command post.

One of the MPs came in. "Your nickname has been changed from 'Dutch' to 'The Butcher.'"

You don't know how close to the truth you've come, I thought, as flashbacks of my days as a doctor at Buchenwald flipped through my mind like still photos. *I feel like I've become as evil as the Germans. What an ugly depressing thought. Do we have to reach their level of inhumanity before we can defeat our enemies?*

That afternoon I interviewed several German soldiers. They were easy to deal with compared to the Nazis.

The last of these soldiers seemed somehow familiar. *Had I met him before? Had he been a camp guard, or served in occupied Holland?* I studied him as I asked routine questions. His familiarity nagged at me.

"Where were you born?"

"Frankfurt."

"Are your parents still alive?"

"Yes." He readily gave me the answers. I couldn't be sure whether it was out of fear of what the other prisoners had told him about me, or whether he was just glad that the war was over for him.

"Where are your parents," I asked.

"They live on a farm near Weimar."

It was like someone turned on my memory switch. "Does your father smoke a pipe? Did your mother have jaw surgery?"

"Yes," he answered, looking puzzled.

The scene flooded back: the farm house, his parents, the kitchen, his bedroom, his clothes, the photos on his wall. I don't know why, but I didn't explain any more to him. "You have very fine parents," was all I said. I figured if he and his parents survived the war, they could tell the story to him.

In my report I wrote; I knew his parents. They helped me during my flight from Buchenwald, and they did not agree with Hitler's philosophy. See that nothing happens to this soldier. After this interview I felt I could take back my old nickname, "Dutch."

In my own small world as an interpreter, I was unaware of the total battle picture, or that the 101st would play an integral part in what would be known as the "Battle of the Bulge." In Hitler's surprise counteroffensive through the Ardennes to reopen a passage to the Port of Antwerp, he had ordered his SS troops to take no prisoners. Alarming reports came into headquarters as the German Blitzkrieg overran the towns of Elsenborn, Saint-Vith and Clervaux, northeast of Bastogne. Hundreds of American prisoners and Belgian civilians were ruthlessly massacred.

American soldiers of the 99th, 106th, 4th and 28th Divisions, outnumbered three to one, slowed the German onslaught toward Bastogne and the Meuse River. But the Germans fought relentlessly westward. Bastogne, a town of 3,500 residents, was strategically important for its central square from which seven paved roads radiated.

On December 18th, Brigadier General Anthony C. McAuliffe, commander of the 101st Airborne, had been ordered to hold Bastogne at all costs. Not until December 20th did we learn that Bastogne was surrounded. Two days of relative quiet followed. The Germans must have been massing troops and supplies for their final assault. Because of the siege and bad flying weather the 101st grew critically low on food, ammunition and medical supplies. On December 22nd the German commander, Lieutenant General Heinz Kokott, sent an ultimatum to General McAuliffe demanding he surrender or be annihilated.

McAuliffe's response, "Nuts!"

One of McAuliffe's underofficers asked me what the German translation was for "nuts."

All I could come up with was, "Go to hell!" This reply went to the Germans.

During these bleak days our garrison's morale was held up only by the strength of McAuliffe, the support of citizens of Bastogne led by their mayor Monsieur Jacmin, and by the distant sound of the III Corps' guns to the south as they headed our way in an attempt to break the siege.

Thank God, on December 23rd the fog lifted and it dawned cold and clear. C-47 cargo planes dropped tons of supplies in the five-mile diameter area around Bastogne still held by the 101st Airborne. From Bastogne's town square other intelligence officers, soldiers and I cheered as hundreds of red, blue and yellow parachutes, coded for food, ammunition and medical supplies, dropped early, desperately needed Christmas presents.

Despite our resupply, German forces made an all out attack on Bastogne on Christmas Day. This assault was preceded on Christmas Eve by a rain of bombs from the Luftwaffe that lit the night into an almost daytime brightness. The ground shook for hours as if we were at the epicenter of a major earthquake. Between bomb explosions, from command headquarters a block and a half from the town square, I heard haunting snatches of "Silent Night." This angelic melody sung by a soldiers' choir drifted from the town's seminary chapel. *God, let us survive this attack,* I prayed in my thoughts. *I don't want to die on Christmas Eve.*

After that night in hell, everyone in the 101st was exhausted to the point of snapping. On Christmas morning, without let-up, German troops fought to the outskirts of Bastogne, just a mile from McAuliffe's headquarters. A Panzer tank unit came in for the kill.

A forward-thinking American Lieutenant Colonel Steven Chappuis, ordered his 502 Parachute Infantry Regiment to ambush the German panzers with tank destroyers from a woods along the attack line. The success of Chappuis paratroopers saved the day for Bastogne and the 101st, and gave the American reinforcements time to close in.

On December 26th, a radio message came from Patton saying he was four miles south of Bastogne. The 37th Tank Battalion, headed by Colonel Creighton W. Abrams, broke through the final miles.

The siege of Bastogne was lifted, the German offensive at the Bulge repelled, four miles east of the Meuse River. By January 28, 1945 the Battle of the Bulge was officially over.

A month later the Germans retreated to their homeland.

CHAPTER XVIII

Voyage to the U.S.

J UST BEFORE NEW YEAR'S Day of 1945, a notice on the bulletin board of our Bastogne bunkroom caught my eye. REFERENCE: ALIENS IN AMERICAN SERVICE: Report to headquarters. When I checked in I was told that the Dutch government had ordered all Dutchmen in foreign services to report back to England.

"Why?' I asked. "Couldn't I stay here? Who would find out? I want to be here to liberate The Netherlands."

"I'd like to help you, Dutch," said my commanding officer. "But there is no way we could get away with it."

Two days later I climbed into a Jeep in Bastogne and was driven to the Port of Ostende, Belgium. When we pulled out of Bastogne, I felt a huge let-down, as if I'd left my best friends. And I didn't think I would ever again serve under a finer commander than General McAuliffe. We'd all become like one big family through the siege of Bastogne and the battles before and after.

From Ostende I boarded a troop transport for England. During the rough crossing of the English Channel, mixed feelings played with my mind. *Why had they removed me from a job where I was needed? What's going to happen now?* On the other hand I was relieved to get away from the fear, noise and bloodshed of the front line.

Upon reaching London headquarters, an official gave me two choices: serve in the Dutch Army with training in England, or join the Royal Netherland Marine Corps and train in the U.S.A. with the American Marines. I remembered Wayne and Tex and other American pilots and all the stories they'd told about their country as I'd led them from Paris to Neuchatel, Switzerland. So I jumped at the chance to go to the U.S.

Near the end of January of 1945, after a three week hold-over in icy Rothneath, Scotland, until thirty-five Dutch Marines had assembled, we were bused to Liverpool, England. As I stepped off the bus, cold, salty-fishy air enveloped me. Squawking gulls glided overhead, distinguishable from the soft gray clouds only by their calls and movement.

At dockside sat the *Queen Elizabeth*. My heart skipped a beat at the majesty of her line. I felt privileged to be crossing aboard her. *Our names will join those of some very prestigious passengers on the ship's manifests,* I thought.

On this voyage the *Queen Elizabeth* assumed duty as a hospital ship. Immediately after bunk assignments, the other Dutch Marines and I carried wounded servicemen aboard from ambulances lined up at the dock. I wondered how the wounded men felt about going home as I looked into their eyes and faces while carrying them aboard. Feeling their pain, I didn't ask any personal questions. Some smiled, despite amputated limbs, lost eyesight, internal injuries and severe burns, seeming to be thrilled that they would soon be back with their loved ones. Many were silent, and a few asked how we happened to be there. It wasn't until 4:00 P.M. that tugs backed the converted luxury liner out of the dock.

As we got underway the ship's Captain announced over the loudspeaker. "The *Queen Elizabeth* has no Navy escort. Our only defense is one gun turret mounted on the top deck. Our best protection is to remain undetected. Keep the blackout curtains closed at all times."

Although there were a lot of medics aboard, they were grateful for the manpower of the Dutch Marines. We rotated shifts. Many of the soldiers had severe wounds, most had to be fed, and some needed assistance with bedpans. I had to carry one patient, a double amputee, to the bathroom. I wondered if he hated the Germans for wounding him. What would he do for the rest of his life? Could he ever live a normal life? I'd never know. I didn't feel comfortable asking him, even after he requested several times that I carry him up to the top deck for a view of the ocean. He probably didn't know the answers to these questions himself.

Occasionally I could sneak up on deck for a walk and a chance to think lighter thoughts. Icy North Atlantic hail crystals pelted my face, but even that felt refreshing after hours spent below deck in the stuffy medicinal wards. I stood leaning on the deck rail watching the mossy green waves curl away from the bow, dreaming of a peacetime voyage on the *Queen Elizabeth*. In the modified but still beautiful dining rooms and salons I pictured myself eating a banquet for every meal. At night I'd take turns dancing with each single woman on board, and wouldn't stop until dawn.

About the third night out emergency bells startled me awake. *A German attack,* I thought, banging my head as I leaped from my bunk.

The Captain's voice came over the loudspeaker. "Man overboard. For the safety of all passengers, we can't turn back. A raft with lifejackets and food has been dropped."

The steady hum of the engines confirmed that we continued on at full speed. Later we heard that a sailor had tripped over some ammunition near the gun turret and had fallen into the ocean. I felt sorry for the sailor, but I didn't know what else the Captain could have done. The Atlantic was full of German U-boats and submarines, and stopping to rescue the unfortunate sailor would have risked all of our lives. Wartime decisions were tough.

The days flew by, and on a clear afternoon of the sixth day we heard the thrilling announcement, "New York City is in sight."

The young soldier who'd lost both legs said to me, "I'm from Kentucky and have never seen the Statue of Liberty. Have you?"

"No." I said. "This is my first time to the United States."

"Would you take me to the top deck."

"I'll see what I can do."

There were only a couple of wheelchairs aboard and both were in use. So I made up a sling out of a bed sheet.

I scrambled to the top deck with my Kentucky friend slung onto my back. Dozens of others joined us. Soldiers opened a path to the rail so we could get the best possible view. Standing up front in the brisk wind, I caught my breath as the Statue of Liberty appeared on a small island to our left. The beauty and freedom symbolized by the magnificent statue made me want to weep.

A sailor next to us started to sing the "Star Spangled Banner." Those who knew the words joined in. My Kentucky friend hummed the song over my shoulder.

It was enough for me to listen and admire the French lady, torch raised in welcome. Even if I had known the national anthem, I couldn't have forced the words around the lump in my throat.

As we coasted past the Statue of Liberty and Ellis Island into New York Harbor I stared in awe at the city skyline. It looked so clean, whole and sparkling compared to the bombed-out cities of Europe. After we'd docked it took less than two hours to unload all the soldiers into ambulances. The *Queen Elizabeth* stood empty. There had been only a little time to say a quick, "good bye and good luck," to the Kentucky soldier and the other soldiers I'd worked with.

The thirty-four other Dutch Marines and I boarded a bus for the Pennsylvania Railroad Station. The sound of honking horns, the smell of exhaust, and the sight of hurrying pedestrians made up my brief impression of New York City as we drove along the streets. Soon we'd reached the station and were loaded aboard a Pullman for North Carolina.

"Here I come, Camp LeJeune," I told myself, eager to become better acquainted with this fantastic country. I figured we'd be in for a long ride, but after traveling in Europe I was unprepared for how long it would take. Distances in America are incomprehensible to a European. That night I was too excited to sleep and watched from my bottom bunk as we passed through brightly lit cities. What a change after almost five years of living behind blackout curtains, covered headlights and streetlamps. I had to pinch myself to make sure I wasn't dreaming.

During the twenty-four hour ride from New York City to ten miles north of Wilmington, North Carolina, the waiters and porters treated us royally. Not being allowed to leave the train wasn't much of a sacrifice. I enjoyed being a spectator of events from the train windows. Even passing through a train stations became an adventure; people crowded around hot dog stands, shops and shoe shine stands. Such a different atmosphere from drab, depressed Europe. I could almost believe there was not a war going on.

On our first morning at Camp LeJeune we received haircuts, physicals and American Marine uniforms with a Dutch patch sewn to the sleeve. Along with more than 1,000 Dutch Marines, I experienced seven weeks of basic training in the tick-infested swampland of Camp LeJeune. I became an expert at backing ticks out of my body with a lit cigarette. The training got tiresome, but we had good food, a bed in a nice clean barracks, and the officers treated us well. It was a thrill to receive my first monthly paycheck of $44.00.

Not until the end of basic training were we allowed to enjoy southern hospitality and southern cooking. I had to agree with the American pilot from South Carolina, whom I'd guided on my fourth trip to Switzerland, that southern cooking was every bit as delicious as he had bragged.

After we'd completed basic training, 120 of us were selected for officers' training and sent to Quantico, Virginia. Training proved tough, but weekend passes to Washington D.C., eased the pain. On one of my first passes, another Dutch Marine, Jacob van Hooten, and I wandered into the U.S.O. building in the nation's capital. A hostess came up and asked us to sign the guestbook.

"Are you two really from Holland?" she asked.

We said, "Yes."

"Tonight there is a benefit dance, and a couple of serviceman from each branch of the service are invited. Would you represent the Dutch Marines?"

"Of course," I almost shouted.

"A limo will pick you up at 8:00 P.M. in front of the U.S.O. building. Have a good time."

My eyes must have gotten as big around as a small boy's eyes on Christmas morning. *A limo,* I thought, *only royalty and movie stars ride in limos.*

That evening, totally unprepared, I walked into the largest ballroom I'd ever seen, surpassing even Queen Wilhelmina's reception room. My eyes almost popped out of my head when I spotted my movie heroes John Wayne, Bob Hope and Dean Martin. And when the big band struck up its music, I found myself dancing with Liz Taylor, Debbie Reynolds, Bess Myerson, Mitzi Gaynor and rubbing shoulders with many other stars. While we danced they asked me questions such as: Where are you from? How did you get to the U.S.? How was it to live under Hitler's occupation? We also talked of less serious things. They joked and flirted as if we'd been friends for years. This had to be a dream.

Tables loaded with food lined the dance floor, and of course I spent dance breaks there. Later that night Bob Hope called all the servicemen to the stage.

"Would you meet and give a huge round of applause to..." and he introduced each of us by name and branch of service. "These two young men represent The Netherlands Marines," he added. In the end we were all given a thunderous round of applause like we were the celebrities. For that night I guess we were.

In the early morning hours the limo driver took us to a hotel.

"Jacob, look at this place. One night here will would cost us two months' pay."

"You can bet on that."

"You'd better leave us at a park bench," I said to the driver."

"The tab will be paid by the U.S.O. Have a good rest and enjoy your breakfast. A car will pick you up in time to get you back to your base."

On our drive back to Quantico, Jacob and I decided not to tell anyone about the U.S.O. dance.

"Who would believe us anyway?" I asked.

January 1945
First arrival in USA

CHAPTER XIX

End of the War

THE 90-DAY WONDER officers' training course at Quantico zipped by. On weekends I visited Baltimore and once took a boat trip around Chesapeake Bay. I made my way through the crowd and found a good place on the top deck. From here I could admire the springtime bloom of the bay area. I filled my lungs with dense salty air, relaxed against the rail and recalled the last time I'd been aboard a boat—the grand entrance of the *Queen Elizabeth* into New York Harbor.

A young man came up beside me and leaned his elbows on the railing. "You must be from Holland," he said, glancing at my Royal Netherlands Marine Corps patch.

"I am."

"Do you speak Dutch, German and French?"

"Yes," I answered, "and also Flemish, Javanese and Malayan."

"Where in the world did you learn to speak Javanese and Malayan?"

"From a school friend named Eddie Visscher whose father worked for the Dutch government in Indonesia. The Visschers would spend six years in Indonesia and then one year at home in The Netherlands. Eddie and his family lived in my apartment building and he and I walked to school together. We became good friends that year. When their year was up Eddie and his family moved back to Indonesia. Eddie and I wrote each other for six years using Javanese and Malayan. I had thought of working in Indonesia when I grew up. His family was due back to Holland to stay another year at about the same time the Germans occupied The Netherlands.

"So you never saw him again?"

"No. After the occupation I never heard from him again."

"So you speak seven languages. That's impressive. I'm getting my Ph.D. in history at Princeton University. I speak German and French. By the way, I'm Sam Chambers," he said, extending his hand.

"Glad to meet you, Sam." I introduced myself.

"I'm here with several classmates," Sam said, nodding toward a noisy group headed in our direction.

Soon his friends arrived and each wanted to try out phrases in German or French. From then on I didn't get to see much scenery, but I had a lot of fun talking with Sam and his friends. They treated me to lunch. Sam told me he was a dealer in old books and handed me his business card.

I licked the hot dog mustard off my fingers, took the card, and slipped it into my pocket.

After his friends had left Sam asked me questions about my family in Holland. I told him a lot about my family, but didn't go into anything about the Dutch or French undergrounds, Buchenwald, Normandy or the Battle of the Bulge. If we ever met again, that would be soon enough to fill him in on that part of my life.

"Have you thought about immigrating to America?" Sam asked.

"Yes, but that would be a long time in the future. I still have to complete my obligations to the Dutch Marines. Anyway, I'd have to have a sponsor and that would be a great responsibility for someone to take on."

By the time we landed, Sam and I were friends. When we stepped ashore he shook my hand. "If you ever need someone to sponsor you, I'd like to be that person. Please write to me. You have my business card."

I went back to Quantico thinking about where I wanted to live after the war. But I wasn't ready to make that decision yet.

Soon I finished officers' training, and two days before graduation discovered I had a bleeding hemorrhoid. My commanding officer asked that I wait for surgery until after the ceremony. I made it through graduation—just barely. After my operation I recuperated in the hospital for seven days and was released. Instead of going home for a two week furlough, which was customary but impossible for me, my doctor arranged for me to spend the time in Detroit with his parents. Ever footloose, I took advantage of this opportunity to see more of the U.S. My doctor's parents were very kind to me. They drove me around the Detroit area, and took me on a side-trip through a tunnel into Canada. Then they let me borrow their car to tour on my own.

On my way back to Quantico, carrying a package for my doctor from his mother, I stopped for a couple of days in Washington D.C. As I roamed the streets early on a Monday morning, someone shouted from an office window, "The war is over!"

I couldn't believe it and ran around looking for a newspaper. Finally I found a May 7, 1945 issue of the *Washington Post*. Sure enough. In tall bold letters the headline screamed, **GERMANY DEFEATED!** It was for real. "This is the best news I've heard in five years!" I shouted to the newsstand attendant.

As news of an Allied victory in Europe spread, thousands of people streamed from apartment houses and office buildings. I found myself caught up in a group of sailors chanting, "The war is over! The war is over!" Each offered me toasts from celebratory bottles. We linked arms and joined the dancing, singing, toasting, kissing, hugging mob running crazily through the streets. After several hours of celebration the alcohol in my empty stomach felt like it would boil over.

That's the last thing I remember until a tap on my shoulder awoke me. A minister announced to me and the dozens of other groaning, droopy-eyed servicemen, "You'll find coffee and rolls in the basement." I tried to orient myself and found I was stretched out in a church pew with the package for the doctor from his mother still beside me. Amazingly it hadn't been lost or stolen during the merriment.

"There will be services in the church in half an hour," continued the minister. I wasn't sure whether he was suggesting we attend or subtly telling us to clear out.

When the church stopped spinning, I went for coffee and a walk outside in the fresh air. Finally my brain clicked into gear. *Now I can contact my family,* I thought excitedly. After a long search I found the nearest Red Cross office.

"We'll try to locate your parents for you," said the Red Cross worker. "Where will you be in the next few days?"

I gave her my Quantico address. "But I don't know how long I'll be there."

I checked back into the hospital at Quantico to be discharged, delivered the package to my doctor and thanked him for the opportunity to visit his parents. The next day I returned to Camp LeJeune. In a less rowdy way soldiers still celebrated our victory in Europe.

The next day our commanding officer's opening statement sobered us up quickly. "We still have a war to win in the Pacific. You'll be trained as part of the forces to land in Japan. An eighty per cent casualty rate is expected."

The bottom fell out of my world. I looked down and blinked back the tears. *Will I ever see my family again, or find out what happened to them? After all that I've been through, I can't even think about fighting in Japan. Especially with little hope of surviving.* In the following days I was forced to face reality because every activity around me readied us for a landing in Japan. I finally convinced myself that Japan had to be defeated and there was no way I could avoid serving there.

Shortly after the announcement to invade Japan, several acquaintances could not handle the news. In desperation one hung himself by a rope from our fire escape. Another faked insanity so convincingly that he was discharged. Neither of these choices sounded good to me.

My next assignment, tank training, took me to Camp Davis, North Carolina. On my first day driving the tank, I jumped in and felt like a young boy learning to drive his first car. In fact I hadn't driven much as a young man. Pa had taught me to drive the car he used for business. But all that had ended with the German occupation.

In the fun of training, I forgot for a while that the purpose was to kill Japanese. As I steered that powerful thirty-five ton tank over the field, I pretended I ruled the universe. I shot the howitzer at imagined enemies, Nazis mostly, and operated the radio. It seemed like a game. With the air-conditioned tanks we trained in a self-contained, seemingly invincible world. The four-man crew and I took turns practicing as driver, gunner, radio operator and tank commander.

Soon after arriving at Camp Davis, I contacted the Red Cross. When they were unable to reach my family, I decided to write home. I never received a reply.

On August 15th, while I still trained at Camp Davis, I heard the astonishing news that two atomic bombs dropped on Japan had ended the war in the Pacific. I was so relieved I sat on my bunk, covered my face and cried. *Now I can plan on having a future,* I thought, pouring out my relief. I sprawled across my bunk, my body feeling as limp as soggy bread. I wiped my sleeve across my eyes. *The death and destruction caused by the atomic bombs must have been horrible. But I think it was justified. After all, Japan started the damned war. If our troops would have had to land, probably more than a million of them would have died.* Every serviceman I talked to that day agreed with me.

Some friends and I celebrated VJ-Day in Wilmington. We joined in the partying: ate, drank, danced and talked. This time I celebrated in moderation, remembering the hard lesson of VE-Day.

What would happen to the Dutch Marines remained a question. Finally we got the word that we would separate from the American Marines, form our own division, receive more training and be shipped to the Dutch East Indies. Unfortunately, the war on that forgotten front was not yet over. In the remote jungles of Malaya and Java, Japanese troops fought on without knowing that the war had ended. While continuing tank training, I took advantage of passes to fly to airbases in Texas, California and Hawaii.

Training ended, and on December 6th the U.S.O. threw a St. Nickolas party for the Dutch Marines. The people of Wilmington, North Carolina made it a very festive occasion. It surprised me that Americans would know about the Dutch tradition of exchanging gifts on St. Nickolas Day. As children we believed St. Nickolas came to Holland from Spain riding on a white horse and carrying gifts. I felt very special about how well we'd been treated by the Americans.

Then on December 8th, 1945, all the Dutch Marines were bussed to Norfolk, Virginia, where we boarded a boat for the Dutch East Indies. It took thirty-one days to cross the Atlantic Ocean, the Mediterranean Sea, go through the Suez Canal and the Red Sea to land in Singapore, part of Malaya. We were put up in tents near the docks.

After our arrival we found out through the grapevine that the British did not want the Dutch in British controlled Singapore, northern Borneo, Timor or Java. Java in particular, was rich in rubber, spices, coffee and tea, and the British hoped to corner the trade on these exports. This issue almost caused a skirmish between the British and Dutch.

The "Dutch beer heist" didn't help matters either. The British had shipped in a large supply of beer for their soldiers and had piled it on the dock and posted guards. I watched several Dutch Marines gather around each guard engaging him in conversation. Meanwhile, other Dutch Marines carried off what they figured was their portion of the beer and hid it under the wooden platforms of their tents.

Right away the British guards noticed the missing cases. Soon the British commander came to see the Dutch commander and I overheard their discussion.

"Your Marines stole our beer from the docks," said the British commander, scowling.

"Did you leave all that beer unguarded?" asked the Dutch commander, barely able to contain a smile.

"Of course not. Three guards were posted."

"I'm sorry, I can't help you." said the Dutch commander. As he walked away he mumbled, "I think I got better men than I expected." He walked to one of his troops' tents and called inside. "Boys, I'm thirsty."

"How about a beer, Colonel?" offered several Marines.

Shortly after that the Dutch Marines were trucked to a deserted barracks at Landang Geddes near Kuala Lampur. Obviously it had stood unused for quite a while—the surrounding wall sagged, and in one spot a gaping hole broke through the fence. That sudden move to Landang Geddes ended the friction between the Dutch and British troops.

To help relieve the boredom before our first mission, some fellow Marines and I went boar hunting in the jungle near Landang Geddes. In the heat two Marines cut off their pant legs and shirt sleeves. Mosquitoes nearly ate them alive. We acted like African hunters creeping through the jungle, our military rifles and carbines at the ready. In what turned into a fiasco, a boar nearly gored a Marine. He'd taken a shot and nicked the boar. The angry boar charged. The Marine quickly braced his rifle against a tree and the boar ran into it's bayonet. Another Marine shot the fallen boar. We rigged up a sled, fastened the boar to it and took turns dragging this crude device. We got lost for several days, ran out of food and ended up eating food the monkeys ate. It wasn't tasty, but it kept us from starving. We ditched the stinking boar. I discovered we'd been going in circles when I found a tree which I'd marked earlier and the tracks from our boar kill. Then someone figured out the directions by the sun. Finally we found our way out of the jungle but had no boar to show for our efforts. Without the evidence we couldn't convince anyone that we'd killed a boar. On top of that no one had even missed us.

Three weeks later our assignment came—rescue fifty Dutch Marines captured while fighting for the French in Indochina and held in a Chinese prison near Peking. My tank unit borrowed twenty ambulances and trucks from the British, and with every available doctor headed up the Malayan Peninsula and the beautiful rural area of China. We drove non-stop for 2,300 miles, rotating drivers as we went. Along the way friendly, poor farmers waved and talked in sign language. We bounced along twisting mountainous roads and in places where none existed made our own.

Ten days later, what I found at the Peking prison sickened me. The Japanese prison camp in China looked like it had been modeled on German concentration camps. All the prisoners weighed less than a hundred pounds and had the same bony faces and skeletal bodies as the prisoners I'd known in Buchenwald. For days, nightmares of my Buchenwald experiences haunted me.

The doctors needed time to check for communicable diseases and to get the prisoners in shape to travel. The Marines were free to explore—I was glad for the opportunity to get away. I enjoyed playing the role of a tourist. We took in Peking, the most unusual city I'd ever seen. The Great Wall of China impressed us so much that some of us walked on it for several miles. As we drove through many villages near Peking, we communicated as best we could with the Chinese people. At night we'd stop at Chinese Army camps where commanding officers gave us lodging, food and supplies for the next day.

After three weeks we returned to the prison near Peking and found the doctors had the prisoners ready to travel. Our convoy then retraced the serpentine route through southern China and Malaya back to Kuala Lampur. On the trip back we cared for the former prisoners and learned that originally 500 Dutch Marines had been captured when Japan invaded China in 1942. In the four to five years they'd spent in prison, only ten per cent had survived the ordeal. A Dutch ship picked them up at Kuala Lampur and returned them to The Netherlands.

Soon after that we returned to Singapore. One night as I walked along a main street I stepped into a bar. As I sipped a beer I heard a familiar voice coming from down the counter. I couldn't believe it. I took my beer, walked over and sat on the stool next to Eddie Visscher.

"Hello, Eddie. Where's that guilder you still owe me?" Just before his family had returned to Indonesia he'd borrowed a guilder to buy a book and in their rush to leave he hadn't had a chance to repay me.

"Jacobus, is that really you? You old son-of-a-gun. What are you doing here?"

We talked long into the night catching up on what had happened in both of our lives since the invasion of Holland. Eddie and his father and mother had been arrested in Indonesia and sent to a Japanese concentration camp. Both of his parents died there. Eddie was released after the war. Though thousands of miles apart through the war, we could share the horrors of our camp experiences as few people could. After that night I never saw or heard from Eddie again.

Soon the Dutch Marines were shipped to Surabaya, Java. On this mission we cleared Japanese soldiers out of the jungles of Java. In their isolation they still didn't realize the war had ended. All except war criminals were sent back to Japan. In Batavia, the war criminals were tried by a British court and given twenty-five to fifty year sentences or death. The Dutch Marines served as guards and executioners. After the atrocities I'd seen in German and Japanese concentration camps, it was not difficult for me to volunteer for the firing squad. It became even easier after I heard that a Japanese Admiral had ordered his crew to fire on a lifeboat full of civilians. On the firing line we were told that only one of us had live ammunition, but from the shape of the bodies after the executions it was obvious that wasn't true.

One evening a prison guard came to tell me about a sick Japanese prisoner. Because I'd seen so much of it, I guessed malaria and took a kit along to his cell. Here I was again acting the part of a doctor, only this time in a helpful way. The man lay shaking like a leaf in a hurricane. My diagnosis was correct. I took his temperature and prepared the needle. I smacked his rear end to get him to relax and inserted the needle. The next day I checked back with my patient. He and his friend stood near the cell door, bowed and called out, "Doctor." I felt so confused, I had to go outside for a walk. One day I'd take a life, the next day I'd save one.

Several weeks later I was transferred back to my tank unit in the eastern part of Java. By then most of the Japanese soldiers had been captured, but now we had to maintain internal peace. Sukarno, a political leader, had taken advantage of the upheaval to gain control of Indonesia. He succeeded and became president of Indonesia in 1945 and remained in office until 1967.

While on patrol in the jungle a few days after I'd returned to Java, an Indonesian jumped out of a tree onto my tank.

"Watch out!" yelled my gunner.

Just in time, I grabbed my gun and shot the Indonesian. He had a poison-tipped knife aimed at my back. I took his knife and scabbard for a souvenir. *When will this all end so that I can go home?* I thought. *I'm so damned sick of being a target.*

That evening I took my frustrations into our camp outside of Lembang, about fifteen miles from Surabaya. When I arrived a Marine told me, "There's no bottled water and we can't drink the village water."

"What the hell do they expect us to do?" I shouted.

I knew what to do. I jumped back into my tank and headed for Surabaya. On the outskirts of town I came to a bridge with a Dutch MP guarding the far side. He raised his hand for me to stop. I was sure he'd tell me, "There's an 8:00 P.M. curfew and you can't come into town."

I didn't care if it was after 8:00, I wasn't in the mood to stop. So I veered to the right, crossed the ditch, drove right through a bamboo house and continued into town. Luckily that house was empty. I'll never forget the look on that MP's face as he leaped to the side of the road. And I never would have believed I'd meet up with that same MP, Fred Berendse, in 1984 in a Knights of Columbus hall in Rapid City, South Dakota. I parked my tank beside a little grocery store. I bought bottled water and beer on credit and charged back to camp. As I roared down the dirt road through the center of camp, the guys cheered and shouted as if I'd single-handedly captured a battalion.

A couple of days later, a messenger came with a note that ordered me to appear at headquarters and answer to these charges: running down an MP, destruction of a house, speeding, and taking beer. I stood before three high-ranking Dutch officials. Eyebrows went up when I told them I'd defend myself. They read me the charges and asked me what I had to say.

"It sounds like I'm going to prison for a long time. But please do me a favor and send me to Buchenwald."

Jack van der Geest and Fred Berendse. Fred was the Dutch MP Jack almost ran over with his tank in Indonesia. They met many years later in Rapid City, South Dakota.

The officers looked at each other in surprise and one said, "That's a death camp in Germany. Why there?"

"I know how to get the hell out of that camp."

"Were you in that camp?" asked the spokesman for the Dutch officials.

"Yes." and I told them the story from the time when I'd been picked up by the Gestapo, to my time in Buchenwald and my escape, through my experiences in the French underground, Normandy and The Battle of the Bulge. "In conclusion," I said, "I fought for freedom and never tried to take it from anyone. Now I'm fighting to take the freedom from the Indonesians. Maybe it's time to give them their freedom. Otherwise I'm a war volunteer, and I'll take my discharge anytime."

An officer asked quietly, "Have you made contact with your parents?"

"I've contacted the Red Cross. But so far they've had no luck."

I was asked to step out of the room. I'd paced up and down the hall only twice when an MP called me in. I stood at attention, expecting the ax to fall.

All three officers stood and saluted me.

The ranking officer said, "We can understand your frustrations. It is no more than right that you should know where your parents are. All the charges are dropped. Your honorable discharge is granted. We will contact headquarters in The Hague to locate your parents. You can have your discharge anywhere in the free world."

I stood there stunned. I couldn't believe my good luck.

Finally for me, the war was over.

From Dutch West Indies into China
to rescue Dutch Marines;
Route from Indonesia back to Holland

CHAPTER XX

Home to Holland

F OR A WHILE I FELT at a loss. My life had been totally restricted and regimented since the occupation of The Netherlands six years earlier. Now I was a civilian in Surabaya, Java, and needed to locate housing, get a job, and do my own cooking and laundry for the first time in my life. I found an apartment on Darmo Boulevard in a former Dutch government worker's house. Then I was hired as a part-time dance instructor in a studio nearby while I waited for my formal discharge.

An English lady lived in the same house. Her husband, a sea captain, traveled on business between all the islands of the Pacific. To keep busy she took dance lessons at the studio where I worked. One day she danced into the studio.

"My daughter is coming from England for a visit, and my husband is returning home soon." Catching her breath she went on. "Will you be home Saturday? I have a big dinner planned and I'd like you to come."

"I'll be there." I was always ready for good food and company.

On Saturday afternoon about four o'clock the English lady came over and knocked on my apartment door. "Can you come over now? My daughter is here and my husband got home early."

I agreed, though I had the feeling she wanted to line me up with her daughter. When I walked into their living room I found a good looking, fashionably dressed young woman. Her mother introduced us. The daughter responded in a heavy English Cockney accent. The mother went on to brag about what a good dancer I was. Then she introduced her sea captain husband. He talked almost as much as his wife.

We sat down for dinner in their dining room. Like most houses in Indonesia this one had high ceilings with fans to circulate the air to cool the rooms. About mid-way through the meal I looked up and saw two chichacs, little lizards, chasing the same mosquito. They bumped head-on. One lost its toe-hold on the ceiling and plopped onto the table.

The English daughter shrieked.

"They're harmless," I said, trying not to laugh too loudly. I picked up the lizard and took it outside.

She relaxed somewhat, though occasionally she'd check on the lizard still hunting mosquitoes on the ceiling.

After that night I was invited for dinner frequently. When the sea captain learned about my language skills and my travel experiences he offered me a job as a station manager for his shipping and transport company in Sydney, Australia Since I needed to earn a living and still had not heard from my family or the Red Cross, I accepted the position. The sea captain's daughter soon left for England and I for Australia. Sydney became my home and Australia my country of citizenship.

Over a two-and-a-half year period I traveled to ports in Hong Kong, New Zealand, India, Indonesia and South Africa where the Captain's ships traded. My job was to troubleshoot when shipments did not arrive on time, when poor quality merchandise had been shipped, or when someone cheated on payments. I also kept track of passenger lists and stocks in the warehouses.

On my first trip back to Surabaya, Java, when I went to the Marine base to finalize my discharge, I found a letter from my mother waiting for me at the post office. I took it back to my local office before opening it. My heart pounded and my clammy hands shook as I tore open the envelope.

Dear Ko,

I have very sad news for you. Your father died in Dachau in February of 1943.

Tears sprang into my eyes. My knees went weak. I sank into a chair and let the letter fall onto the desk. Thoughts tumbled through my mind.

My father, my idol, was dead. There was so much I should have said. Pa, I wish I had told you how much I loved and respected you. Now it's too late.

I propped my elbows on the desk and sobbed into my hands until I felt emotionally drained. I leaned back in the chair and stared unseeing out of my office window.

Pa, you were such a good man, such a hard worker, always looking for ways to better yourself and our family. Life was never easy for you. You had to go to work at an early age because you were the oldest in a large family. You educated yourself. You worked your way from an errand boy to the president of a bread factory by age forty-two. I hope you can hear me now and know how much I cared for you. I want you to be as proud of me as I am of you.

I slowly picked up the letter and read on.

Your sister Willie and brother-in-law Koo are fine. They hid in the house of Koo's parents for the entire occupation and survived several surprise searches.

Ko, when are you coming home? I never doubted that you were still alive. I never gave up hope. I knew you were too slick for the Nazis, and I was right.

I'm doing fine. Write and tell me when you can come home.

Love always,
Mother

I read between the lines that Ma was very lonely. Immediately I went to the telegraph office and wired her:

I'M OK, RECEIVED YOUR LETTER, WILL WRITE TODAY.

As I traveled the South Pacific I thought a lot about going home and about where I would like to settle down after that. Though I wanted desperately to get back to Holland to see my family, I knew I didn't want to stay there. More and more often, memories of my days in the U.S. came back to me. One day as I checked through my wallet I found the business card Sam Chambers had given to me on the boat ride on Chesapeake Bay. By now he might have forgotten me or changed his mind. I took the chance and wrote to him anyway.

On my next stop in Java, a second letter from my mother awaited me. This one was not as depressing as the first. I responded right away, telling her I'd like to see her as soon as possible, that I'd made up my mind to settle in America and that now everybody called me Jack.

Back in my office in Sydney a letter from Sam sat on top of my mail. I stared at the air mail envelope for a full minute. My future rested on the words written inside. Finally I took a deep breath, slipped my finger under the seal and slid it across the flap.

> Dear Jack,
>   My sister Alethea and I would be honored to be your sponsors. Come as soon as possible...

I felt like leaping onto my desk and shouting my news to everyone in the office—to the whole world. Instead, I stuffed the letter and my trembling hands into my pockets and went for a walk. No one could understand my feelings at this moment. As I strolled the streets of Sydney my emotions ranged from joy, to uncertainty, to fear.

I remembered meeting Sam on the Chesapeake cruise. I thought about my surgeon and his family and the many friendly people I'd become acquainted with while in training and during my travels. I pictured myself living a wonderful life with my own family and friends just as I'd seen in American movies. I felt certain that America could give me many more opportunities than I could ever have in Holland. With each step I felt more confident that I had made the right decision.

I did not sleep that night. Early the next morning I went to the Emigration Office to see about a visa to America. They informed me that there was a four-and-a-half year waiting list for an Australian citizen to emigrate to the U.S.

"I'd have to wait four-and-a-half years to go?" I asked incredulously.

Later when I found out from my mother that The Netherlands had a six year waiting list, I was so discouraged I wanted to disappear into the Australian outback for days. I had no one to talk to about this problem. God, now what am I supposed to do? I did not give up. When my mind wasn't occupied with business, I thought about what other country would give me a visa to America.

One day as I cruised toward Indonesia, a brilliant idea popped out of the blue sky. *Indonesia,* I thought, *why not try Indonesia? No one there saves enough money to emigrate. I'll bet there is no waiting list. And I already speak the language.* The minute I arrived in Djakarta, Java, I checked with the American Embassy.

"There is no quota for Indonesia," said the American worker behind the desk. "Most Indonesians don't have enough money to buy shoes, let alone to emigrate anywhere."

"What can you do for me?" I asked, handing him Sam's letter.

"Nothing," he said, giving back the letter. "You were a Dutch citizen, now you're an Australian citizen. I only work with Indonesians."

I thanked him and went to an Indonesian government office. "What does it take to become an Indonesian citizen?" I asked the native woman who waited on me.

With raised eyebrows she looked me up and down. She seemed surprised that a tall, fair person from a northern European country could speak Malayan so fluently. She left without comment and returned in five minutes. "It takes a thirty day stay in the country and knowledge of the Mayalan language."

"Thank you," I said. "I have some unfinished business in Sydney, but I'll be back."

I leaped from the chair and ran out of the building. *At last I've found the solution!* I shouted in my mind. After sending my resignation to the Captain, I finished up my two weeks and flew back to Djakarta. On my return to the Indonesian government office, I talked with the same woman as before.

"This is day one," I told her. "Do I have to report in every day?"

"No, that isn't necessary. Just give me the address where you'll be staying."

I gave her the local address of the boat company manager where I'd arranged to stay. While waiting for my thirty days to pass, I helped the manager in his office.

On the thirtieth day I walked into the government office. The same woman handed me a citizenship paper already filled in with my name. Paper in hand, I returned to the American Embassy and showed it to the same man who had rejected me earlier.

He smiled. "Anyone who goes to that much trouble to get to America deserves any help I can give him." Immediately he began to process my papers. "Would you like to stop in Holland on the way?"

"Yes. For three months if possible."

"I'll contact the office in Rotterdam, and when you arrive they will stamp your pass and you can be on your way."

I couldn't believe it. This was all happening so fast. I'd gone from despair of ever reaching America, to having a sponsor, citizenship papers and an American visa. Thank God, again. My dream had come true!

I contacted the Dutch Marine base commander, who was now one of the three officers who'd sat at my court martial hearing. He recognized me and gladly arranged for me to return on a troop transport. I wired Ma and Sam telling them I was on my way. Two days later I boarded the *Kota-Inten* and, along with 700 Marines, headed for Holland.

I'd hoped for a smooth, problem-free voyage home. But the last leg of my trip home proved to be every bit as frustrating as getting to that point.

We stopped in Batavia to pick up 1400 Army personnel, filling the ship to beyond capacity. Two days later as we cruised on the Indian ocean, the Captain's voice came over the loudspeaker.

"Everyone must report to the dispensary for smallpox vaccinations. I will call you alphabetically. 'As' go now."

The Dutch Marines had had their shots. The Army contingent had not. The military men became unruly with concern. Not until then did the Captain inform us that two cases of smallpox were being treated in the ship's hospital. In a short time it became evident that shots given after exposure to the disease were ineffective. More soldiers entered the hospital every day. One of the original two patients died, and his funeral was held the same afternoon. I watched his body slide into the sea.

The next day the crew roped off part of the ship to isolate the smallpox patients. Every day the cordoned off area grew on each level, and every day the number of funerals increased.

I felt sad for the soldiers and their families. To serve their country for so many years, then to catch smallpox on the way home was rotten injustice. It became too depressing to attend all the funerals. I just wanted to huddle in the farthest corner of the ship away from the infected patients.

Thank God I'd been ordered to get a smallpox vaccination before my visa was issued. Soon it became apparent that even this was no guarantee that I would not become infected. After a while even Marines who'd had shots came down with smallpox and died. As more and more of the ship turned into a hospital, I walked around in a panic thinking that I might be next. I couldn't eat. I couldn't sleep.

The *Kota-Inten* docked at Aden, a British port at the south entrance to the Red Sea. Three hundred patients were unloaded and taken to a hospital. Our ship continued its voyage. A yellow flag flew from its mast, warning other ships to stay away. We passed through the Suez Canal and into the Mediterranean Sea. This should have been a joyous time-we'd reached the spectacular Mediterranean, the back stretch on our homeward trip. But soon after unloading the smallpox patients in Aden, men continued to come down with the disease and the hospital again filled up.

Finally, after two nightmarish weeks, we arrived in Holland. The *Kota-Inten* coasted into the port of Rotterdam on a clear, beautiful Sunday afternoon.

My throat tightened and tears welled in my eyes at the familiar sight of Rotterdam Harbor. I'd spent almost seven years away from home. How could it have been so long? It was all I could do to resist the urge to jump overboard, swim to the dock and run all the way to The Hague.

Military boats surrounded us, keeping our infected ship isolated. Are they going to keep us aboard until the epidemic has run its course? Then I saw a string of buses and ambulances lined up at the dock, and I breathed a sigh of relief. Before long MPs in white helmets escorted the healthy men onto buses.

On the ride through Rotterdam I approached the driver. "You can let me off here. I'll find my way home."

The driver pointed his thumb toward the MP, standing at the door.

"He'll never let you off the bus."

In resignation I sat down. "Where are you taking us?"

"You're going to a camp to be disinfected."

After a couple of hours the driver slowed. "We're almost there." He drove through a gate.

When we passed through that gate my stomach knotted and I felt like I would vomit. I leaped up, ran at the MP and tried to force my way past him. He and three Marines grabbed my arms and pinned me down.

"Don't send me back there!" I screamed. "Don't send me back there."

We'd stopped at the first concentration camp where I'd spent the night in a cattle car waiting for the train to leave for Buchenwald. I felt like I would go crazy—electric shocks danced around in my brain. I kicked at the MPs and flung my arms around trying to shake them off.

Finally they subdued me and dragged me to a cell. I was locked up and left alone. I paced like a caged tiger, beat my fists on the bars, and yelled and swore at the guards to let me out. Several hours later, finally exhausted, I lay on the cot. Soon, two MPs led me to the commander's office.

He stood. "Several assault charges have been filed against you."

"Are they military charges filed against a Dutchman?" I asked, looking him directly in the eye.

"Yes," he answered.

"In that case you better let me go. Now I'm an Indonesian civilian. And in 1942, when I was nineteen, I visited this camp before being taken to Buchenwald."

The commander relaxed his military stance and sat down, indicating for me to do the same.

"Tell me what happened."

When I'd finished talking, he said, "That's one of the most incredible damned stories I've heard come out of the war. You were scheduled for disinfection Friday. I'm going to arrange to have it done now."

After my clothes and I had been disinfected, I returned to the commander's office. A black staff car decorated with flags pulled up outside.

The commander shook my hand. "Have a good stay with your

family, and good luck in America."

At last, I thought, as I sank into the leather-seated comfort of the car, *I'm on my way home.*

CHAPTER XXI

Reunion

I CLOSED MY EYES and rested my head against the soft leather seat. *Would Ma recognize me after all these years? Would she be different after all she'd been through?* I sat up and nervously ran my hands down my pant legs, trying to flatten out the wrinkles in my disinfected but unpressed pants.

My heart banged in my chest as we pulled up to our old apartment house. The building looked a little neglected, but otherwise pretty much the same. I glanced up at our third floor apartment and noticed that Ma had hung our red, white and blue striped Dutch flag in the window.

I jumped out, asked the driver to bring my duffel bag and sprinted for the entrance. Taking the stairs two at a time I arrived breathless at our door. After sucking in great gulps of air I rang the doorbell.

Ma opened the door. "What do you need? Can I help you?" she asked, a confused expression on her face.

"Ma, can I come in?" I reached out to hug her, but instead had to catch her before she fainted.

"Ko!" she said. She threw her arms around my neck. "I saw the staff car," she said between sobs. "I thought a man from the Dutch government had come to tell me you were dead. You weren't supposed to be here until Friday."

Ma and I talked almost nonstop for three days. I let my mother tell her story first.

"After we were separated," Ma began, "I didn't know where you and your father had been taken. I ended up in Ravensbruck. It was a living hell, and with my arthritis I was nearly helpless. I wouldn't have survived without a lot of help from the other women. There was no heat in the buildings. I put on everything under my clothing that I could find-newspapers, rags. But still I was cold all the time. I was so miserable I almost ran to the fence to get it over with. Days passed by, and every day became more unbearable than the last. And for the younger women it was worse. Soldiers took them away, and they came back all beaten up. At least I was too old to be bothered with.

"You could tell by the soldier's faces which ones were mean. One day, after about three months in camp, I noticed a new face. I recognized the soldier immediately. He was the German soldier who had come to our house to pick up Willie for that blind date Rieta had arranged. I felt desperate, so I tapped him on the arm and asked if he remembered me.

"He said 'No,' and shrugged off my touch.

"When I reminded him that he had been to my house in Holland to pick up my daughter for a blind date, he looked at me closely. He said he remembered and asked what I was doing here.

"I explained how Rieta had fabricated a story to get us in trouble. The soldier must have had some authority, because the next day I was called in, released and sent back to Holland. When I got back home I found out from neighbors that Rieta had gone to Vienna to have a baby. After the war she was tried and given five years at hard labor. By then her husband had returned with the Navy from England. He'd shouted out at the trial that five years at hard labor didn't begin to make up for her crimes.

"Enough of Rieta. Now a couple of months after I was freed from Ravensbruck, on February 27, 1943—I remember that date exactly—a German soldier knocked at our door. He gave me a notice that said to report to German headquarters downtown the next day at 10:00 A.M.

"I walked around our apartment the entire night worrying that I'd be sent back to prison. The next morning I dressed in double layers, just in case.

"When I walked into headquarters my knees felt so weak I thought I would fall. Soon a soldier took me to a private office. The officer behind the desk asked me to sit down. He picked up a paper, came around and sat on the top of his desk. He was a young man, could have been my son. I sat there stiffly. My muscles ached from sitting so straight. I watched him closely as I sweated in my warm clothing. He fidgeted around, then finally spoke. He said he had bad news.

"He got up, walked behind his desk, sat in his chair and told me that my husband had died at Dachau on February 19th."

I took both of Ma's crippled hands in mine and held them so she could go on.

"It was difficult, but I asked the young soldier where my husband's remains were. He said your father had been cremated and the remains would be sent to me after the war. He handed me the death certificate.

"I don't remember how I got home," my mother continued. "My whole world had caved in. After that I managed the best I could. I worried constantly about you, but I kept up hope that you were alive. Occasionally I'd heard from Willie and Koo during the war while they were at Koo's parent's house. After learning of your father's death I went to visit them. Willie was scared, but all right. So at least I knew they were safe.

"There was no end in sight. For a long time all the war news was bad—Europe had been occupied and Italy had joined the Nazis. We could hear American and British planes flying toward Germany, and German planes headed for England but didn't know what to make of it.

"Food became even more scarce and the curfew was moved back to 6:00 P.M. One day in August, after curfew, I heard a knock on our door. I opened the little window in the door and saw the skeletal face of a concentration camp survivor. The skinny man said,

'Mrs. van der Geest, may I come in? I'm a friend of your husband.' I thought, *what do I have to lose*, and let him in.

"He introduced himself and started to talk. 'It was about three weeks ago when I escaped from Dachau, and it took me several weeks to get back here.' I told him that I'd received notice six months ago that my husband had died, and showed him the death certificate.

"He said, 'That's a lie. I saw him three weeks ago. His feet were swollen to twice their size and bleeding badly. His weight had gone below one hundred pounds. But he was tough, wouldn't give up for anything. That's why he was consistently being punished. Of all the men I've met, I remember him best, and always will.' I thanked him for coming. After that night I never saw this man again.

"I paced all night thinking about your father. Could he still be alive? Was he in pain? In February I had put my mind at ease thinking that he was not suffering anymore. Now mixed-up feelings ran through me again.

"Soon after this man's visit a period came where many people passed away. Both your Grandmother and Grandfather van der Geest died within a short time. Living became almost unbearable. Only the hope of finding you alive kept me going. Then we heard about the landing at Normandy in June of 1944, and we were ready to hang out the Dutch flag. But the Allies could get no further than Nijmegen. Life became miserable again.

"You know what gave me reason to live? Two members of the Dutch underground contacted me in September of 1944, and asked if I would hide an American navigator who had parachuted from a plane shot down near The Hague.

"I told them to bring him over.

"One of the underground members returned and converted our closet in the back bedroom into a hiding place. He left a loose board in the floor so the navigator had a crawlspace in which to lie down and hide. I closed the trap door, set down a newspaper and put my shoes on it as if they'd been left to dry.

"The next day they brought Dave Smith to me. The underground trained us in case of an SS search and occasionally brought us extra food. We were left on our own. His uniform was dirty so I gave him some of your clothes. He couldn't understand Dutch and my English was not much better. We communicated through gestures and drawings. He drew a map of the U.S. and showed me that he lived in California. It took several attempts for him to explain to me that he worked for the Game, Fish and Parks Department as a fire watchman. For entertainment we taught each other every card game we knew. In the daytime he'd stay in the house, and at night we'd sit on the balcony to get fresh air. The underground had told us to expect an SS search. I kept an eye on the street. Sure enough, one day I saw a couple of military trucks parked at the end of our block. The SS started a house-to-house search. I called to Dave, 'Hide.' I lifted the trap door, and Dave got in. I shut the door and set out the newspaper and placed my shoes on it. I checked to see that there was no more than one cup or plate out. A knock came on our door. Two German soldiers aimed their guns at me and asked how many people were inside. I said, 'just me.' One soldier ordered me to go downstairs and wait. Everyone on our floor stood outside. I didn't show any emotion and tried to calm them down. They talked about the four Americans who'd parachuted down and were in hiding. One said, 'I don't know why the SS are searching our building. The crew couldn't be here.' About a half an hour later the German soldiers came downstairs without Dave Smith. I

Dave Smith and Jack's mother

sighed inwardly, knowing that if they'd found him I would also have received a bullet. Three weeks later the SS searched our apartment building again. And again we survived the search. I kept Dave hidden for nine months, until the end of the war.

"On May 5th, 1945, when the Germans surrendered, Dave Smith ran to the front window, swung it open and yelled, 'We are free!'

"I hung out our Dutch flag.

"Our neighbors were shocked when they found out he'd stayed with me for nine months. In fact the rest of his crew also survived in hiding. Before he left I had a ring made for him out of silver coins. When I talked to a jeweler about making the ring, he said he was making another coin ring for the woman who'd hidden the pilot of the plane which had been shot down. I told him my ring was for the navigator of that plane. He was so impressed that he made both rings for free. Through the jeweler we contacted the rest of the crew and Dave met with them soon after. When Dave Smith left for America we agreed to stay in contact. He said he would write and send food packages. I was very saddened to hear that he died in an automobile accident soon after he returned to America.

My mother got up and walked to the dresser and opened the drawer. "Look," she said, and lifted out two medals. "General Eisenhower and General Montgomery came to our apartment and gave me these medals for keeping Dave Smith in hiding. Photographers took pictures and reporters asked me lots of questions."

I hugged Ma around the shoulders, "I'm proud of you, Ma. Pa would be too."

Ma looked at me wistfully, tears in her eyes. "Do you think your father is still alive and was sent to a camp in Siberia?"

"Only God knows," was all I could think of to say.

Over the next few weeks I told Ma my complete story. We cried and laughed, sharing our grief and joy.

I visited my sister, Willie, and brother-in-law, Koo. Although they were glad to see me, my sister only talked of the present and future. She refused to speak of or listen to one word about the past.

To earn extra cash during my three month visit, I translated for a Dutch inventor. In my free time I tried to contact old school friends and managed to locate a few. I felt buoyed up whenever I got together with an old friend to relive fun times. But then when I found out from friends of the Cohen family that all of them had died in concentration camps, I felt depressed. I realized life in Holland would never be the same. It was time for me to make a fresh start.

All too soon my departure date arrived. Emotional family ties tugged at me to stay in Holland, but reason and my adventuresome spirit pulled me toward America.

"Go," Ma encouraged me. "You will never be happy in Holland."

Now I could go without guilt. I had my mother's blessing and my sister's promise to take care of our mother. Ma and I took the train to Rotterdam.

"I'll come visit you," I said, "and you can come to see me in America."

I hugged Ma and boarded the *Veendam*. I waved to Ma until I could only see a tear-blurred dot on the dock.

On November 5, 1949, I started across the Atlantic to begin my new life in America. My deepest hope and prayer was that God would never again take an extended vacation as it seemed He had done during World War II.

Even more, I prayed that mankind with his God-given gifts of intelligence, foresight, and compassion would take the responsibility to see that a World War II and a Holocaust would never happen again.

1951
United States Air Force
B-36 Radar

Married
January 7, 1952
to Elaine Kollars

Afterward

UPON JACK'S ARRIVAL in Baltimore, Dr. Sam Chambers and his sister Alethea met him at the railroad station and brought him into their home. Within days Jack took a job as an electrician at a German-owned electric company. He found it ironic that after his experiences in a German concentration camp, a German man was the first to give him a job in America.

Several months later Jack rejoined the service, the Air Force this time. Following training at Lackland AFB, Texas, and radar school at Keesler AFB, Biloxi, Mississippi, Jack was stationed at Rapid City AFB in South Dakota.

On May 5, 1951, Jack met Elaine Kollars at a U.S.O. dance in Rapid City and they married in January of 1952. On May 5, 1953, Jack became a U.S. citizen. A son, Van, was born to Jack and Elaine in 1954.

Jack's mother came to America for a visit in 1956. When Jack picked her up in New York, driving his new, financed car she commented, "My gosh, only seven years in America and you're already a millionaire?" His mother was also surprised that it took more than one day to drive to South Dakota.

Jack and Elaine made trips back to The Netherlands in 1974, 1982, and 1986. While there they traveled in Germany and to other European countries. Several times they tried to get Willie to join them in their travels, but she said, "I will never set one foot in Germany as long as I live." Jack and Elaine enjoyed traveling in Germany. "The people were friendly and pleasant," said Jack. "One couple gave us the use of their bedroom for a week." When they talked about the war, some Germans agreed that what their countrymen had done was wrong. Jack's last visit to Holland was in 1992, when Koo, his brother-in-law, died.

After leaving the Service Jack sold cars for several years, then went into the insurance business. Throughout his years in Rapid City, Jack gave of his time and talent in return for what America had given to him. He belonged to the United Commercial Travelers and served on the board for six years. He was first chairman of the West River Chapter of the American Red Cross, active in the Knights of Columbus and acted as Master of the Fourth Degree for South Dakota. Jack is past president of Life Underwriters Association, past president of the Amateur Radio Operators, member of the Rotary, life member of VFW, the Elks and Moose Clubs.

Jack has shared his concentration camp and war experiences with middle school and high school classes in North and South Dakota, Colorado, Wisconsin, Minnesota, and Wyoming. He has spoken at meetings of the Rotary Club, Optimist Club, Kiwanis, teachers groups, many reunions of Army combat soldiers, Air Force and Marine reserve groups, and various civic groups over the western two thirds of the United States.

In June of 1996 Jack's beloved wife Elaine died of cancer. Jack told his son that Elaine's death was more difficult for him to cope with than all of his camp and war experiences.

More than a year after *Was God on Vacation?* had been published, in April of 1997, Jack received a telephone death threat.

The male voice asked, "Are you the writer of *Was God on Vacation?*"

"Yes."

"Are you Jack van der Geest?"

"Yes."

"If you know what's good for you, you better take your book off the market. Otherwise you'll be history." The caller hung up.

Jack called the Rapid City police. They put one detective on the case, and notified the FBI as is necessary in all death threat cases. They recommended he get caller ID, have mirrors put in and around his house, and that he keep vital phone numbers handy.

Ten days later another call came. The same voice said, "If you don't know what it means that you'll be history, it means we're going to kill you." The phone went dead.

Jack turned the phone number indicated on caller ID over to the local police. They traced the call to a convenience store pay phone in Box Elder, SD.

A third and so far last call came on November 1, 1997. The same voice said, "You still have your book on the market. You better take your book off the market or we'll kill you." Again the caller hung up.

Jack feels sad that even in this country with so many freedoms, he must look over his shoulder.

Jack is now retired from the insurance business, but he is more active than ever on the speaking circuit. He spoke for the second time to Doug Peterson's history classes at Eagle Butte High School outside of Rapid City. The following summer Doug Peterson traveled to Germany and Buchenwald. He asked to check the archives, and using Jack's camp ID number found a copy of Jack's death certificate that said that he had died in March of 1943. Doug made a copy and sent it to Jack. After this Jack talked to his insurance man, the company president. "Here's my death certificate. Can I collect on my policy?" He was told, "No. You were already dead when you bought the policy."

Jack was also interviewed by the Shoah Foundation. The foundation, sponsored by Steven Spielberg, is an organization dedicated to preserving the remembrance of those who experienced the holocaust first-hand. Jack's video taping lasted almost 8 hours to cover his amazing story.

Jack's latest adventure, in November of 1998, was a trip to Japan sponsored by the Rapid City, North Dakota, Chamber of Commerce. Since his run-in with Japanese soldiers and war criminals

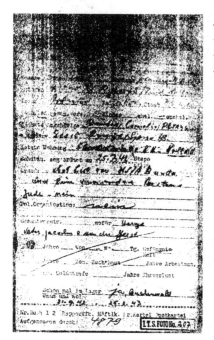

Jack van der Geest's official Death Certificate from Buchenwald. Died March 3, 1943.

in China and Indonesia in 1946 he'd harbored resentments towards the Japanese people. Now he's resolved these feelings. Just as he'd gained understanding of the German people on his visits to Germany, he's gained that same insight into Japanese people on his trip to Japan.

Jack continues to travel and speak, and visits Colorado regularly to spend time with his son, daughter-in-law and two grandsons.

"I'm grateful for all the years that I've lived in the United States. I have never gone hungry. I've had a good life. But my thoughts are often with the young boys who hit the beaches of Normandy, France, in June of 1944. They gave their lives to liberate the nations oppressed by the tyranny of Hitler's troops. Also I've never forgotten the American soldiers who fought in Korea and Vietnam. They've all made it possible for us to live in a free country.

"Next time you pledge allegiance to our flag, I hope you get the same thrill down your spine that I do."

Anne van der Geest
(de Groot)
Jack's mother
1956 visit to America

Jacobus van der Geest
Jack's father
1942 —Two weeks
before he was taken to
Dachau concentration camp

Bibliography

Aubrac, Lucie. 1993. *Outwitting the Gestapo.* Nebraska: University of Nebraska.

Blumenson, Martin. 1978. *Liberation, WWII.* Virginia: Time-Life Series.

Crookenden, Napier. 1976. *Dropzone Normandy.* New York: Charles Scribner's Sons.

Fry, Varian. 1945. *Assignment Rescue: An Autobiography.* New York: Scholastic.

Gilbert, Martin. 1989. *The Second World War, A Complete History.* New York: Henry Holt & Co.

Julitte, Pierre. 1971. *Block 26, Sabotage at Buchenwald.* New York: Doubleday & Company, Inc.

Keegan, John. 1989. *Second World War.* New York: Viking

Samelson, William. 1989. *One Bridge to Life.* Maryland: Clark-Davis Publishing Co.

Skipper, G. C. 1982. D-Day, World at War Series. Chicago: Childrens Press.

Time-Life Books. 1989. *World War II.* New York: Prentice Hall Press.

ten Boom, Corrie. 1971. *The Hiding Place.* Ohio: The Christian Library, Barbour and Co., Inc.

Wiesel, Elie. 1982. *Night.* New York: Bantam